Emotional Maturity Series

What Happy People KNOW

The Path of Emotional Maturity

Volume II

Chuck Spezzano, Ph. D.

Edited by Eric & Celia Taylor

Cover design by Guter Punkt, Munich
www.guter_punkt.de

Printed and bound in Great Britain by
CPI Group (UK) Ltd, Croydon, CR0 4YY

ISBN 978-1-907798-28-3

Dedication

To the Prior clan –
Evie, Tony, Hollie, Robert,
Lizzie and Charlie.
Thanks for your true hearts
and a home away from home.

Acknowledgments

First of all, I would like to acknowledge the inspiration that makes these books possible. It is a gift given to me and I receive it as best I can.

I would like to thank my wife for her love and support through this book and so many others.

And my beautiful children who are an inspiration and support by the love they give and engender.

To my team, Charlie and Napua, for handling the details, allowing me to write.

To Sunny, my typist, a heartfelt thanks.

To my editorial team of Eric and Celia, I have much gratitude for your good eye, our friendship, and the wee dram we share when we get together across continents.

A Course in Miracles has been an ongoing influence in my life, bringing me peace and understanding. This book is built on much of that understanding.

And a blessing and special thanks to you, my dear readers, without whom I would be a bridge to nowhere.

Contents

Introduction

I was never very good with my emotions. They always seemed to 'blow me away' like a hurricane. I really had to learn from scratch how to handle my emotions. I made all the mistakes of repression, dissociation, wallowing, feeling sorry for myself, controlling, fighting with my emotions, using them to get attention or for revenge, and finally for specialness. But that didn't work at all as I certainly wasn't happy. So I began to learn about emotions, what they were and how to handle them. I learned to face my fear enough to give up my independence and go for partnership. You need to relearn these principles every time you have an emotional reaction, because that is just what an emotion is – a reaction rather than a response. The emotion seems out of control, and you seem out of control in regard to the emotion that is running through you. It is important to learn not just to control yourself, but also to learn how to return to peace and wholeness, and that can only be accomplished through healing yourself and learning to catch yourself quicker when you are reacting. Awareness and the desire to begin the healing process as soon as possible are what is needed. You might as well learn these principles and begin your path of healing because it is the way to being true to yourself, recovering your heart and being a great partner. Sound enticing? Read on.

Emotional maturity is what brings partnership and flow into your life. Maturity does not misuse emotions for specialness, as weapons, or to indulge yourself in a manner that sabotages relationships by making everything about you. Emotional maturity focuses your energy toward giving yourself fully and toward your purpose, both of which bring joy to you and to the world. If you use your emotions in an untrue way, the gifts that would have naturally emerged to meet the challenge are aborted. When emotions come up, it is because something has tripped your defenses and the pain beneath them. You are at a crossroads. Will you use it to defend the ego or will you use it for truth and greater success? Pain is not Heaven's Plan for you. Heaven leads you on a path home to happiness. Everything is part of your curriculum but if you resist and try to do things your way out of fear, then the control leads you into conflict. The way becomes difficult because you do not recognize Heaven's grace that is given to you to make your way easy.

> Perhaps you have misunderstood His Plan, for He would never offer pain to you. But your defenses did not let you see His living blessing shine in every step you ever took. While you made plans for death, He led you gently to eternal life.

A Course in Miracles

Emotional maturity makes you open, attractive and true. It is a gift to your partner and those around you that invites greater partnership and flow. Rightly used, the energy of your emotions transforms into positive feelings used to live your purpose and contribute to life. As you become more centered, it adds to your self-value and the goldenness you radiate. If you misuse your emotions, you block grace and the help Heaven wants to give you every step of the way. You do not let grievances, which are always attached to emotions, stop your life from progressing. Emotional maturity is emotional integrity. It is this integrity that adds to your wholeness, and this allows you to receive life's bounty.

Without emotional maturity and the partnership it brings, you will never be true to yourself. You will build your ego but not those aspects that build real joy and happiness, such as love, purpose and your destiny. To be true to yourself is to realize you are not the ego and its self-concepts, which are built on pain, fear, guilt and separation. Want something more for yourself. You are not your body as your ego tells you. You have a body, which is a great learning and communication vehicle. If you think you are your body, you will soon be on a downhill slope toward death and this builds the ego as much as aggrandizement. Beyond your ego is your limitless spirit, made of light and love. Don't be caught by problems, the fabrications of the ego that hide fear of going forward. Self-concept by self-concept, your ego melts away with love and forgiveness, and there is less of who you think you are and more of Heaven. Your life shows all that you have achieved. It also shows the impediments and limitations of who you think you are. Let's see, do you want that, or more love and the happiness and freedom that come with emotional maturity. Hmmm. Which direction will you go? What do you want? What will you invest in – the truth or the pain the ego told you was the truth? Emotional maturity brings the peace that brings health, abundance, love, joy and finally eternity, once the last wall of the ego fades away.

Common Misconceptions About Emotions

1. At the present time most people are frightened of their emotions and don't know what they are for. No one likes to feel emotional pain but if you do not know the true purpose of your emotions, the ego tends to hijack them, using them for its own ends, which merely increases separation and builds more pain.
2. People think emotions come from the outside: "She hurt me" or "He made me angry", "That made me sad" or "Work frustrated me", "I had no choice in how I felt". Emotions actually come from thoughts, values and choices that influence how you choose to react to outside occurrences.
3. People think happiness comes from the outside, and it does come from the outside somewhat, but those circumstances that made you happy, change. People are forever trying to get happiness from outside themselves. This becomes another form of looking for love in all the wrong places. It is the happiness from within that is lasting, not that which is dependent on outside circumstances. It is when circumstances change that emotions come up.
4. "My partner *should* love me. That's what a partner is there for." People feel justified in getting angry or showing other forms of tantrum because of what happened and how it affected them. This is tantamount to saying, "When people break my rules, I have a right to be angry. If they don't abide by my rules, I will punish them." You are demanding obeisance to your specialness and you want your partner and others to feed your needs by keeping your rules.

5. "Avoid pain at all costs!" Pain is an indicator of what needs healing. To avoid it would be like avoiding a poisonous snake in your house. It's a good short-term strategy but the snake needs to be dealt with so you don't find it curling up in bed with you on some dark night. Each emotion can show a whole pattern that needs healing.

6. "Complaining is harmless. It is a way of letting off steam." Complaining is a form of attack that states someone outside of you should be making you happy. It is an attack and a self-attack that lowers confidence. It is trying to get the world to change. Yet, it is your change that makes you peaceful and happy.

7. "Complaining and nagging are good ways to get what I want at work or at home." "The squeaky wheel gets the grease." When you nag to get something, you don't feel worthy of it because you had to bully or manipulate to get it. This can set up a vicious circle of nagging and lack of self-worth.

8. "It is natural to judge those who are bad or who act badly." To judge is to put yourself in sacrifice to what you have judged. You think the judgment puts you above what you have judged and separates you from it. Both judgment and separation generate pain. You do nothing to another that you don't also do to yourself. You judge those you are actually called to help, forgive, bless and even save from themselves. To judge is to reinforce the hidden guilt that led to the judgment.

9. "Pre-emptive attack is justified to protect myself." To the ego, attack is a way of life. You attack even those you love the most but, as attack is not discrete, you attack yourself and everyone else to the same extent. This sets up a world of pain. The ego attempts to prove the need for its existence by fights. It makes itself bigger through conflict and war.

10. "I don't know why bad things happen to me. Bummer karma probably..." You use the subconscious and unconscious mind to hide that your life is as you have chosen it to be, and that you are a co-maker of your world.

11. "I get angry or hurt by others' behavior. How people act is not my responsibility." Yet others who seem to be upsetting you are actually acting out your script, hidden under the one in which they seemed to go against your wishes. This is a reflection of your split mind and the hidden self-concepts you have projected out on those around you. How others act proves you are the best and most special of people, not like the others. You believe your judgment of others proves your superiority and specialness.

12. "What I see and experience is exactly what is happening out there. I'm a passive receptor." Perception is a choice and what occurs, even when negative, serves a purpose for you, one that you hope to gain some pay-off for. Ask yourself what you are using an event, experience or perception for.

13. "I try to distract myself from emotions. Bad feelings are to be avoided at all costs." Distractions simply put off what must be dealt with. It would be like putting to sea in a leaky boat. If you plug the holes before you set off you can enjoy the ride.

14. "What is going on in my partner has nothing to do with me. When they are in a bad mood, I walk quietly or try to avoid or ignore them. Their emotions are their problem." This is acting as independent, in sacrifice or as a victim. Actually, everything in a relationship is collusion and the world mirrors your mind.

15. "I'm stuck with the emotions and actions in people around me. I'm helpless to change it." Yet the world is your mirror and as you change your mind, you change the mirror. You could ask yourself what you are using this experience for.

16. "I cannot be upset unless someone doesn't do things my way." Rules are meant to be broken and rules are defenses that call for attack and bring about what they were meant to prevent. If you exchange your rules for principles, you will dialogue a lot more and suffer a lot less.

17. "I am not responsible for my emotions. They are just how I feel." Only your thoughts can hurt you. It is your misinterpretation of events that leads to pain and brings about thoughts of pain. As you change your mind about an event, it can dissolve fear, loss, sadness, hurt, heartbreak, guilt and grievances. The reason emotions can be healed is that they are ultimately untrue.

Chapter 1

The Power of Catharsis

To release your emotions heals you. Feeling your feelings and melting them away is the simplest form of healing. Once all the pent up emotion is released, there is a new birth. If you have an illness, injury or problem, the release of all the emotions surrounding and driving it leads to the next chapter that this issue was distracting you from. The release of emotions melts away the fear of the next step and there is a renaissance as a result.

All of your problems have pent up emotions as their basis. If instead of judging or being afraid of your emotions you let them go, it would bring sweet release, leading to tenderness and poignancy. You would regain your heart and a new level of bonding and understanding. You wouldn't be held back by suppressed or repressed emotion. The space where the emotion was would become available for self-love and receiving. You wouldn't use your emotions as a weapon or for manipulation. To release all the emotion would be to heal the needs involved, dissolve the guilt that attaches itself to any saved up emotion and to end the resistance that builds up.

To release painful emotions as they come up is to learn the lesson that brought them about so you can be certain of inoculation against similar mistakes in the future. To release an emotion as soon as it comes up is to regain and expand your heart and to glean wisdom from the release of suffering. Wisdom does not come from suffering. It comes from the release of emotional suffering. Suffering that is saved up just gives you post-traumatic stress. To save up emotion separates you from yourself and everyone, locking you in the triad of independent-victim-sacrifice roles that stops partnership and receiving. It is important to get into a right relationship with your emotions so you don't exaggerate them in hysterics, which avoids the crucial emotion that needs to be dealt with. On the other hand, it is also crucial not to dissociate your emotions, which cuts you off from them and hides them inside as if you had finished with them. Use either of these defenses and it blocks ease, partnership, authenticity and receiving. You are then neither free nor true to yourself. The beauty of catharsis is that it redeems and refreshes your feminine side so that the more you let go of your emotions, the more loveable you experience yourself to be. Paradoxically, as your needs are fulfilled by letting go, there is more of you that you can share. This also increases your love and happiness.

When you feel you experience a pain that is too overwhelming, there is a tendency to 'disconnect up' or 'disconnect down' in order to dissociate and protect yourself from being overwhelmed.

When you disconnect up you ostensibly become more spiritual but it carries a hidden or not so hidden superiority and even arrogance. You feel above the common herd and don't want to stoop into the pain of the world or its venality because it would open the pain you cut yourself off from. This is the darkest part of disconnecting up because usually people who do this seem fine and spiritual.

Then there are those who disconnect down. They cut off the higher chakras and throw themselves into the pain of the planet. These people can be earthy and sexual. They can also be 'slimy' if they try to assuage their pain through greed or sexual avarice. On the positive side, those who disconnect down could move into law enforcement or into the healing professions to handle suffering. They are typically hard workers but they can also burn out or be overwhelmed with the vast amounts of crime or pain they deal with. Things can get dangerous for them if they burn out emotionally or feel overwhelmed by the pain around them. At times, approaching the higher realms and chakras that they have cut themselves off from can make them feel bereft of what they have lost. Or they shy away from the pain and so they would rather dissociate this aspect. They may feel the higher reaches are not for them even though they don't quite know why.

Those without that earthiness have disconnected up and are quite sensitive to pain and stress. They can easily become overwhelmed or overworked, while those who disconnect down can at times accomplish prodigious amounts of work and bullet through the pain. The split of these two major aspects is one of the main ways the ego builds itself, because the ego comes from such separation.

Almost everyone disconnects both up and down, and sometimes a number of times. If we do this too much or with great magnitude, we can become schizophrenic. Usually this disconnection simply dissociates us.

In a relationship, if one partner disconnects down, the other typically disconnects up. This leaves vast amounts of pain between them. If you join your partner by feeling the pain between you, leaning into the most acute part of it and stepping forward while remembering Who walks with you, there would be a renaissance in the relationship and a great release of post-traumatic stress as you join your partner. There would be a new level of success and intimacy. There is a great deal of pain between partners who have disconnected up and down and it takes courage to join, yet the renaissance available is quite powerful. Each time you come together to join these opposites, a new wholeness, effectiveness and power come about. It is only the deep love for a partner who has disconnected in an opposite way that leads you through the pain to join again and again, and recover yourself.

Recognize whether you have the tendency to disconnect either up or down. What does your partner do? If you are different, it can typically become one of the judgments that you have on each other unless you appreciate the complementary nature of your relationship, or until you finally fully join and become whole. If you are not frightened of the pain between you but value your partner and love them more than the pain, and if you realize they need your help, then you will lean into the pain until you can join them heart to heart.

If you are doing this joining for yourself because you don't have a partner, you can commit to the side that you are presently cut off from, whether it is disconnecting up or down, and lean into the pain until both sides join in wholeness. Keep committing to this part of you until you feel a greater balance and a new level of integration between these aspects of yourself. Invite love in where there was this split in your mind. This will have a positive effect on your ability to partner, allow greater ease and ability to receive, and provide a new chapter forward in relationship.

Today, do not be afraid of the pain that you have carried around with you as a wall between you and life. Step into the pain with Heaven's help and wade through it in love to your partner, yourself and those closest to you.

Chapter 2

To Feel Guilt is to Punish Those You Love

To feel guilt is to punish those you love. When you feel guilt, you automatically punish yourself. This attack and the withdrawal that comes from guilt not only affects you, it also affects all those you love. All minds are connected, and even more so those closest to you. Since attack is not discrete, the attack on yourself becomes an attack on those you love. Those you love can't stand to see or sense someone they love attack themselves. They experience it as painful and an attack also. As *A Course in Miracles* states: "You never crucify yourself alone."

So, to protect those you love from suffering, you must embrace your innocence. If you experience yourself as innocent, then you will also experience those around you as innocent. If you see yourself as worthy of condemnation, you will see those around you as deserving condemnation and punishment.

Innocence is freedom and by espousing the path of innocence, you commit to your freedom and the freedom of those around you. Commit to your total innocence and that of all humanity.

Chapter 3

To Feel Guilt is to Punish Yourself

To feel guilt is to punish yourself. To feel guilt is to feel that you have somehow failed. This is an emotion that is almost impossible for anyone to live with. So, in spite of how much guilt you seem to have, most of it is repressed. You then project it out on others and the world but this doesn't free you. It only seems to get rid of it, but it is still locked inside you. You simply deny that it is there. It actually doesn't matter whether you hide your guilt or are completely aware of it, you still punish yourself.

When you feel you have failed yourself and those you love, you feel compelled to attack yourself to try and get some relief from the guilt. The pain of self-attack is distracting but it in no way clears the guilt. As a matter of fact, when you attack yourself, you feel bad and feeling bad is one of the descriptions of guilt. So feeling bad because of your self-attack only leads to more guilt and more self-attack. Guilt is its own vicious circle that spirals downward into even greater feelings of failure. Guilt is a terrible illusion that adds great suffering to the earth. And it is not just yourself that it affects; you withdraw from those you love and you judge others because you also see them as worthy of punishment. Punishment does not help you learn the lesson – on the contrary it reinforces the mistake.

To learn the lesson and correct the mistake, you must turn to the principles that free you from guilt, such as forgiveness, innocence and love. All these bring compassion and the atonement that corrects mistakes and builds greater relatedness.

Today, for the sake of the truth, for the sake of those you love, for Heaven's sake and your own, practice forgiveness on everything that upsets you. Forgive others and yourself. Every hour ask who you are called to forgive. Forgive them, yourself and God. Think back to every painful thing that ever happened to you. Forgive yourself for planning such an event to punish yourself, forgive the event, forgive those you used as an instrument to punish yourself, and forgive Heaven because anything you blame on anyone you blame on Heaven.

Now it's time to help yourself and the world to be free.

Forgiveness is a practical form of love.

Chapter 4

Your Emotions are Blocking What You Want

Your emotions are blocking what you want. Emotions fill up the space in your mind and heart where you would receive love, abundance, recognition and even health.

Becoming aware and letting go of these emotions are the keys to opening the door to be able to receive once more. Set your intention to find what is in the way of success in all these areas. You might consider choosing one area at a time, such as your relationship or your health. Commit to finding the emotions that are in the way. When the emotions that are upsetting you begin to come up, it is important to remember that you asked for them. Since emotions are by choice and are not determined by something outside you, it is better to recognize and release them, rather than have them eating away at you and filling the space inside your mind that was meant for love and confidence.

Unless you are a person who has to go through every emotion and feel it until you are completely clear and peaceful, there are other easier options. Here are a few:

One is to simply imagine that there is a flow of grace inside you washing away the emotion.

Another, which has been a favorite of mine recently, is to imagine yourself bringing whatever emotions you are experiencing to Heaven's Trading Post. This is open 24-7 and gives trade-in for the illusion and pain that you have in the place meant for peace and success.

A further way is to forgive yourself and each emotion, and anyone who comes to mind regarding the emotion, until you are in a state of peace.

A fourth way is to realize that each of these emotions is keeping you emotionally arrested in the past, which is why you can't receive in the present. As you commit to the next step, you can leap over these emotions. Once you are past them, the defense for the ego that they provided is gone and the emotions are naturally re-integrated.

A fifth way is to imagine each emotion melted down to its pure energy and integrated into your higher mind.

These are ways to let go of emotions that are in the way of your receiving. Heaven's intention, and that of your true will, is to receive every good thing, as opposed to your ego, which keeps itself strong by pain.

Chapter 5

Awareness about Emotions is Crucial

Awareness of emotions is crucial. Your emotions are the currents and sandbars in the river of life. If you don't know them, you can get swept away or stuck. On the other hand, some people never venture out or go in the river no matter how hot it gets. As emotions are the number one element that determines your behavior, they set the very tone of your life. If you are not aware of your emotions, you don't know where the alligators are waiting in the tall grass, ready to bite your ass.

It is important to know that you have emotions that are hidden inside by denial and dissociation. Beside the emotion itself, there is also a cache of guilt and fear that goes with each one. To be happy and successful in every area of your life, it is crucial to become aware of these caches of emotions in order to clear out every dark place in your mind. What isn't cleared out attracts equally negative events and problems.

The extent of your independence, a form of dissociation, is the extent of your hidden dependence, pain, need, fear, guilt, sacrifice and where you felt victimized. Your independence merely compensates for them. Yet, until you are at the highest stages of enlightenment, you continue healing caches of emotions from subconscious and unconscious levels of the mind. These emotions are at the root of all of your problems, so to heal them before they grow into problems is most helpful. Being aware of emotions and releasing them before they become health, money or relationship problems, to name but a few, can stop many a rude awakening. Be proactive about becoming aware and healing when it comes to your emotions; it will save a lot of pain and the difficulty of doing things the hard way. You will like yourself better and have an easier time of it.

Chapter 6

In Any Painful Situation There is Something You Could Give to Make It Better

In any painful situation there is something you could give to make the situation better. While there are a few general principles that are helpful in any problem situation, you might start by asking what you could give and to whom. I have found that you are never in a situation in which you don't have a gift that would remedy it. You could open the door in your mind for that gift and receive it for any problem or situation you are in. The gift is typically a powerful soul gift, waiting for this problem to motivate you to open it.

There are some general gifts to make a situation better and they may be specifically called for in your situation. All problems come from fear. This problem generates delay and distraction so you won't have to face the fear. But love heals fear. It is the opposite of fear. It melts the effect of being frozen that fear brings. Forgiveness heals fear. It is a giving forth of what is needed to heal the fear of inadequacy that keeps you afraid of moving forward. It frees you from the paralysis of fear. Peace heals fear, as fear is a lack of harmony, and peace dissolves the illusion that feeds it. Trust heals fear, restoring your confidence. Your mind has to invest in something. It will either be worry and fear, or it will be trust. Trust is putting the power of your mind toward a positive outcome. Fear is putting your mind toward an illusion and dark fantasy that you can make real to yourself if you keep investing in it. Giving yourself fully in commitment heals fear as this rejoins you in bonding and there is no room for the fear.

What could you give energetically that would heal the problem? If it is a problem situation or a chronic problem, then you may need to give something every day, as the problem may involve a number of relationships, both past and present, that need correction. You could bring these gifts to these relationships and thus move the situation back into the flow.

Chapter 7

Fear is Always a Fear of Inadequacy

Fear is always a fear of inadequacy. When you are afraid, you are afraid you don't have what it takes to handle the next step. Both fear and inadequacy begin with loss of bonding. Because you feel inadequate, you feel you need something outside yourself to bolster you up. You are afraid you can't do it. When you lose bonding, you disconnect from yourself, others and from Heaven. Then you go looking outside yourself for what was inside you all along, but you fear that you won't get it because you aren't good enough. If your mind wasn't split between wanting what you want and doing things your way, which you have confused with the true way, you would have what you wanted easily, naturally and quickly. There would be no split mind and no conflict between your goal and the hidden desire for independence. Your split mind makes it extremely difficult for you to receive because you want two things and what you have shows what you want more. The feelings of inadequacy are the insurance the ego uses to keep itself separate.

To heal fear means to face what frightens you. Healing is the strong intention to go forward in spite of the fear. However, when you feel inadequate, you feel you can't go forward on your own. You shrink back from life and become unwilling because you think you are not up to whatever awaits you. As a result of this fear of inadequacy, many times you compensate and, as a result, you work too hard, try too hard or push yourself too much. However, the compensations are no more effective than shrinking back.

You could let go of your fear. You could reconnect with yourself and Heaven and this would have you reconnect with those around you. You could integrate your fear and feelings of inadequacy, together with the defenses and compensations you use to hide these things, by choosing to give them to your higher mind. It will accomplish the integration for you. This will create a new confidence and wholeness. It will set up a new willingness and flow. It will open new relatedness to yourself, others and God.

Chapter 8

Your Strategy for Getting is Defeating You

Your strategy for getting is defeating you. It does this in a number of ways. First of all, no one likes to be taken from. As you take, you build up resistance from those around you. The more you do it, the more they begin to resist and move away from you.

Getting and taking are ego remedies in response to the pain, fear, guilt and split mind that comes as a result of the loss of bonding. The ego dissociates the pain, guilt and fear for you but doesn't take it away, as the ego builds itself with these emotions. Because of your split mind, you both want what you want and don't want it, valuing the dissociated independence of your ego more.

Finally, as you get and take, you increase your fear that someone will get and take from you. The extent to which you get and take is the extent that you become vulnerable to someone taking from you. In addition, your getting and taking builds up guilt so you eventually get yourself punished for getting and taking. All of these ways are painful and self-defeating. If you restored your bonding, you could simply receive instead of trying to take. If you gave instead of trying to take, you would naturally receive for your giving. What you take you don't really feel worthy of and, as unworthiness builds, you start pushing away the good things in your life.

Taking and getting reinforce the common mistake that it will be something outside of you that either saves you or makes you happy. This is one of the root causes of both emotional immaturity and pain.

What you give, you receive and what you try to take, you lose, but it is your choice. One path brings power struggle and heartbreak and the other path brings love and fulfillment.

Chapter 9

Being Emotionally Arrested Comes From a Past That You Haven't Gotten Over

Being emotionally arrested comes from a past that you haven't gotten over. Through some painful event, a part of you stops and doesn't grow up or go forward in life. As a result, you have wounded children driving the truck of your life. Those on the sidewalk had best look out. In these places you are reactive rather than responsive and if you have too many of these, you become a bully, frightened, neurotic and controlling. These arrested parts are programs inside you that set up further heartbreak and defeat. In each of these places, you have a split mind. It is as if the wires in your heart, mind and body were cut. This can lead to ill health, poor energy and a depressed outlook. Wherever you have a problem, you have an arrested self inside you.

The good news is how easy it is to heal these wounded, arrested selves. Choose a problem. Ask yourself how old is the wounded self (or selves) that is at the root of this problem. See those arrested selves inside and pour love to them. Imagine yourself holding them and comforting them. As love fills them, they will once again begin growing up until they reach your present age, at which time they will melt back into you, reconnecting the wires in your heart, mind and body.

Now, do this with the biggest trauma of your life. Ask yourself what effect your wounded selves within have been having on you. Love yourself until you are completely healed and happy once more. This is an excellent exercise to revisit as needed.

Chapter 10

An Expectation Demands the Very Thing You Are Not Giving to Yourself or Others

An expectation demands the very thing you are not giving to yourself or others. If you were giving it, you would never demand it. Instead, you would simply ask for it. When you invite someone to do something, there is an excellent chance they will do it. But if you expect or demand something of another, there is a good chance they won't comply. And if they do, they do so under duress and sacrifice rather than freely choosing, so it is not satisfying.

If you gave something to yourself, you would not expect it from another. If you gave that thing to others, you would be satisfied and have no need of demands. When you demand or expect something of others, you are out of integrity. You have a split mind because you broke away from bonding. This makes you frightened that you won't have your need met, the need that comes from the broken bonding. But on the other side of the split mind you are frightened you will get the need met, and that bonding will be restored and you will lose your independence. Consequently, you act in a manner most calculated subconsciously to have the other not succeed in giving it to you freely. You are out of integrity with yourself, acting against yourself and your own best interests.

It is untrue and out of integrity to expect of others what you are not giving. If you have what you demanded, you would be free and it would seem less important, whether someone complied with your wishes or not.

As you let go of expectations and demands, they become no big thing and it is likely that when the urgency dissipates your wishes are more likely to be acceded to.

If they aren't, it is no big thing. If you have an expectation, it is always a big thing.

Success comes from letting go of the expectations, demands and the needs that fuel them. Success comes from giving to yourself and others. Then there are no demands. It is then you can receive, because the split in your mind that shows as an attachment is gone.

Chapter 11

Fear is Always a Fear of Loss

Fear is always a fear of loss. When you are afraid, you fear you will lose something. Both fear and loss begin with lost bonding and, as such, set up a vicious circle until bonding is restored. After losses in the past, you anticipate losses in the future, and this is what fear is – that the future will be like the past. This is only transformed when you have the courage to let go of your past and future. This opens you to the present and the possibility for a new beginning.

Whenever you chose separation you chose to lose and were willing to experience the loss in order to have your independence. When you make such a choice, albeit one you hide even from yourself, there is a good chance you underestimate the effects that the pain, loneliness and loss will have on your life. In spite of the ego's dissociation, you not only have the pain, fear and loss, you also have a pattern of victimization. Naturally, the plan to go independent at the price of loss is something you deceive yourself about and blame life or God or another for. Being aware of this brings back your power and insures you against making the same mistake again. If you lack awareness and attack another and yourself for your mistake, you will be caught in the denial and destructive role of the victim.

Letting go of loss, and the attachments that are meant to compensate for loss, creates an antidote to fear. You depend on whatever you are attached to outside yourself and this contains fear of loss. To let go of attachments is to help remove victim patterns and enhance bonding. Where there are attachments, there is dependency and fear. This puts whatever you are attached to at risk.

The law of attraction is such that if you are afraid you will lose something, it actually attracts and programs the loss. Luckily, there are other positive influences that can hold what you are afraid of at bay, but the best option is to let go of attachments until there is re-bonding or love without need.

Whenever I would get ready to leave home for work-travel, I would recognize my attachment by the sadness that would come up a day or two before I flew out. It was then I would practice letting go by putting my wife and children in God's Hands. Paradoxically, once I let them go, I felt they were safe and I could leave, feeling centered.

Your fear is an illusion. It is a fantasy that something negative will occur and, when it occurs, you will lose something of value.

It is time to let go of your illusions and fantasies. It is time to let go of your doubts and worries. Fear attacks life and it attacks you. Instead, when these fears come up, ask yourself who you are called to extend love to. This extension of love re-bonds you and this will have the positive effect of melting away your fear and giving you confidence. If more fear comes up, simply repeat the exercise.

Whenever you have a problem, know that one of the core dynamics is fear, which is fear of loss. In any problem, ask yourself what it is you are afraid you would lose if the problem was resolved and you moved forward. Let this go and you will move forward without the fear of loss. Help someone who needs your love and you will similarly move forward, melting away the fear with your help.

Chapter 12

Fear and Inadequacy Feed Each Other

Fear and inadequacy feed each other. They set up their own vicious circle. When you feel one you also experience the other, and they reinforce each other in a downward spiral that leads to a place where you shrink and paralyze yourself. The more fearful and weak you become, the more inadequate you feel and this makes you more likely to attack others.

Both fear and inadequacy begin with lost bonding and they lead to following others blindly, holding back, or trying too hard. Perfectionism, with its stress and inability to relax, comes from attempting to compensate for fear and inadequacy. Perfectionism can trigger off comparison, one of the great sources of pain in life. It can also trigger off the vicious circle of superiority-inferiority. Both are inextricably locked together making you feel above or below others but never allowing you to relax and enjoy. Superiority is simply a compensation. The Snob and the Groveler shadows are opposite sides of the same coin.

With fear and feelings of inadequacy, you either give up or drive yourself relentlessly. You drift, or push yourself, or both. Love heals fear and inadequacy. Forgiveness heals fear and the feeling of inadequacy. Remembrance of Who walks with you heals fear and inadequacy. Trust, the choosing to use your mind for a positive outcome, heals inadequacy.

Letting go heals fear and inadequacy, as does understanding. Realizing that fear and inadequacy are attempts to build your ego and keep you from the sacred promise of your purpose allows you to choose again. Both fear and inadequacy are based on self-concepts that attempt to hide your identity as spirit.

When you realize that fear and feelings of inadequacy are emotions that you use to keep yourself away from others, you could choose to join instead.

Fear and feelings of inadequacy are not the truth and you can invoke the truth rather than invest in these illusions. Commitment heals fear and inadequacy because the old splits in the mind that generate and feed fear and inadequacy disappear more each time you give yourself fully.

Chapter 13

Problems are a Complaint

Problems are a complaint. They are a complaint that someone didn't take care of you the way you wanted and your problem has occurred because of this.

A problem in your life says that someone else, but not you, is to blame for what is going on. This falls under the category of the biggest mistake in life, which is that another is responsible for your experience and your happiness. This makes relationships full of anger because you refuse to take responsibility for yourself and what happens to you. If you were to see into your subconscious and unconscious mind, you would know that you were completely responsible for your whole life.

Problems are a form of self-attack. You are willing to do this to yourself because somehow the complaint to and about the other is that important to you. It may be that you are afraid of your power and don't wish to take responsibility for your life. Or it may be your need to prove someone is a 'bad guy' and you, on the other hand, are so much better. Complaints attack your self-esteem in that they state you don't have the power to help yourself. Problems are always a form of avoiding your purpose and identity as spirit.

To give up your complaints, it is necessary to take back your power and use it to transform the situation. You can forgive the other, yourself, the situation and your beliefs that led to it. You can take responsibility for your life and make a difference. When you realize that all guilt is solely an invention of your mind, you also realize that guilt and what is necessary to save yourself must both be present in your mind. You could choose to help yourself and others instead of blaming yourself and the inevitable complaining about others that goes with it. In understanding this, you are saved.

Your conscious mind has a nasty tendency to cut off and hide what doesn't fit your picture of yourself and others. When there is guilt, it has the unfortunate result of wrongly condemning and cutting off some very important pieces of your wholeness.

Also, even if the fantasy present in every demand is granted, it comes from a need. If bonding doesn't occur, there is no real satisfaction and you then make another fantasy that you hope will satisfy the need inside you this time for sure. But, it is not expectations, demands or fantasies that meet your needs; it is relatedness. It is your dedication to greater relatedness that finally satisfies you and gets you over the emotions of fear and inadequacy. Then you are no longer falling into the biggest trap of expecting something outside yourself to satisfy you in life or relationships. It is the relatedness itself that not only meets your needs but also fulfills you. Whether you connect to another or not is up to you but only this will work to heal and make a difference in your happiness. This is because happiness comes from your decision to relate more and more, while unhappiness comes from your decision to separate, and this shows up in every victim situation. Do you want to complain or do you want to find that you have the very gift inside you were complaining you didn't get.

Chapter 14

A Major Problem Hides Major Denial

A major problem hides major denial. Problems and victimizations are the result of denial. You hide from yourself what is really going on. This is not unusual because you naturally want to think positively about yourself and don't want to see what it is that you have done or the mistaken choices you made. You hide these mistakes from yourself and this is what made both the unconscious and then the subconscious mind. You have so much power and so many gifts buried inside but these are stopped by the denial you have. If you allowed yourself to see what you were doing, you could make another choice. You wouldn't choose to repress things. You wouldn't decide something subconsciously; you would want to see all that was hidden in your mind. These caches of darkness contain pain and guilt. They program problems, and are what traps and sabotage are made of.

It is time you changed your mind and to do this you have to see what is in it. Everything in your world reflects what is in your mind. Everything that is occurring happens as a result of the choices you are making. Let yourself in on past mistakes so you can correct them. Let yourself see what is in your mind so you can change it if you don't like it.

If you don't like what is in your world, you can commit to seeing what is in your mind that it reflects. But to see what is at the root of your present situation, you must be willing to look deeper and see what is really going on. Now is the time to commit to finding what you have hidden from yourself. If you commit to finding all the hidden caches of darkness within, your higher mind will bring it up to you, step by step. Then you can turn it over to your higher mind to undo it with grace. Commit to give up self-attack. You have been punishing yourself for what is inside you. Now is the time to forgive yourself, acknowledge your mistakes and get on with your life. A new world awaits you. You can win back your power and your gifts. You can shine your light and have the life that you want. Be dedicated to finding what you have hidden away from yourself. Remember, mistakes can be corrected. When you see a mistaken choice, you can choose again.

Chapter 15

Your Defensiveness Fights for an Illusion

When you find yourself becoming defensive, notice that what you are defending is not real, but some ego illusion. Would you rather have love or your self-concepts? You have become defensive because you felt alone and weak, but you don't realize that this is a choice on your part. It may have been a choice you made, but you can choose once more. Nothing between you and another is stuck, if you are willing to overlook it. What makes it seem impenetrable is some sort of specialness and self-concept you are defending. If you are willing to change and see things more maturely, you and whomever you feel hurt and angry with can go to a new chapter together.

If you invoke truth, the illusion cannot withstand the force of it. Nothing between you will seem impenetrable any longer. If you are willing to forgive your partner, then truth and a healing perspective will come. In the long run, you will be happy that you did not lock yourself into a painful and defensive stance because you felt so alone and weak, and that you did not delay yourself with conflict.

Follow the emotion that has come up. Ask yourself where it began and you will come to a root event where the pain began or was compounded. It is here that forgiveness dissolves the root. It is here you felt so alone and victimized but it is also here that the gifts and purpose you turned away from still await you. These gifts are big and would allow you to shine so much more. This is what whoever you have been defending yourself against needs.

Step up now. Heal yourself now. The change is just what will bless and free you. Your happiness depends on it.

You need never be reduced to feeling alone, weak and separate. Remember Who it is that walks beside you.

Chapter 16

If You Are Hiding, Life Will Give You a Hiding

If you turn away from life, it seems to turn away from you. If you are afraid of life, yourself and your purpose, you cut yourself off from what you need. You swim upstream against the flow of life. You go against the Tao. You think you know better than the Holy Spirit, who only wants what is in **your** best interest.

Hiding is an aspect of your ego but it goes against your true nature and your own self-interest. Your ego is interested in itself. It is not interested in you, though it tells you that it protects you. For instance, it assures you that it protects you from your purpose, which it swears is too big for you. Of course, your purpose is too big for you but it is not too big for you and Heaven, which the ego wants to separate you from, telling you that you are on your own and have to do everything yourself. When you turn away from Heaven and grace, your workload increases 100%.

The second meaning of 'hiding' here is a whipping or a spanking. When you are hiding, life will give you a *hiding*. You are turned away from the light and turned toward the darkness of the ego that leads to death. You are going in the wrong direction and cutting yourself off from inspiration. You have judged against yourself, life and Heaven.

Ask yourself now the percentage that you have been hiding. Recognize the scarcity, problems and issues of your life demonstrate where you have turned away from the light and are hiding.

Make a new choice. Let Heaven empower your desire to stop hiding and step up. Put it all in Heaven's Hands. This is Heaven's job. Your job is to recognize your mistakes and make a new decision, so your will is aligned with Heaven's Will, which is for you to have every good thing. This is not your ego's will, which wants to stay strong at any cost, but it is your true will to be free.

Chapter 17

Anything Can Be in Service to Help You Get Your Heart Open

Anything can serve to help you get your heart open. Of course, every positive thing in life is there to help you feel love, gratitude and appreciation. It brings you into the here and now where there is only love. Those around you who need your help can open your heart with compassion. But even what hurts and makes you angry or leads you to feel bad, if used correctly can be a way to help you recover your heart.

The attitude necessary to help you regain more of your heart when you are upset is to realize it shows a place where you have lost love and thus a part of your heart. A negative emotion or incident shows a place where you are making a mistake inside but also where you could correct it.

If you take responsibility for what you feel and what happens to you, you can change it. Realize it is an opportunity and ask where the root of it *began*. Forgive everyone in the original situation. Forgive yourself for your mistaken choice, forgive the one you made a scapegoat of, and forgive the situation itself. Ask yourself what gift you turned away from to follow the ego's path of separation and control. Ask what gift of Heaven you refused, as well as the purpose and destiny you ran from. Be willing to receive the gifts, embrace your purpose and destiny and share them with those in the past. Then bring your forgiveness and gifts into the present, sharing them with whoever or whatever upsets you now. As a result, feel the love and heart that is added to you in your life now.

Chapter 18

It is Important to Check in With Yourself

It is important to check in with yourself. It is important to know when you have become lost or gone off the track so you don't go on and on in a negative pattern. You should review your day each evening, before you retire. Where did you lose patience? Who were you angry at? What left you upset? These places show you where you have something from your past attacking your present. They are there to delay and distract you but, if you realize that you could just commit to the next step to move past any fear of going forward, you would be fine. Then you could use your review to learn the lesson you missed. You may have blown an opportunity to have learned a lesson the easy way but there really is no problem, you can learn it now. Simply beware of guilt or self-attack, which is an ego ploy to keep you from learning the lesson, and taking advantage of the opportunity now.

How old were you when the negative feeling that came up today actually began in your life? Who did it begin with? You can go back to this point with your mind. You can feel each emotion till you reach peace and then a new beginning. You can forgive each person, yourself and the situation, both now and then, until there is peace.

You can go deeper. Recognize that you wrote the script. Besides attacking another and yourself, and besides separating for independence, what was the next step in intimacy or success you were afraid of? What were you being right about? What were you trying to get? You were afraid to embrace the soul gift, Heaven's gift, your purpose and destiny in each of these situations. You can do this now as it would create a major course correction in success and love. You would shine that much more and have ease instead of tribulation. The worse the pain is that you are experiencing, the bigger the gift within. As you heal in deeper and deeper ways, you pull out the radiance of gifts that accompany your destiny, which is who you came to be. This radiance is success with effortless effort. It comes from your *being*.

Chapter 19

Attack is an Attempt to Make Up for Inadequacy

Attack is an attempt to make up for inadequacy. When you feel weak, you attack. It is an attempt to equalize the situation. In the old West the revolver was called the 'great equalizer' because the size of the man didn't matter if he had a gun. When you attack, you don't feel up to the task of communicating. You don't feel you have what it takes to be heard, so you attack in order to bring someone down and raise yourself up.

Your attack is an attempt to control another and have them do it your way to meet your needs. If you felt good about yourself there would be no demand, control or manipulation, there would only be invitation, which has a much better chance of success. Anything won or taken from another may get you what you want, but it will not confirm your 'loveableness' or be the response that fulfills you.

Attack, by its nature, unequivocally states that the other is both guilty and not worthy of love. In effect, it states the same thing about you when you attack, though consciously you feel righteous and morally superior. Attack attempts to place you above another, winning the competition and proving that you are the best by whatever means of force the attack is made up of.

Attack does not increase your confidence. On the contrary, it engenders greater separation, fear, competition and lack of safety. It reinforces the very inadequacy it was an attempt to heal.

Attack and self-attack are the very foundation of the ego. Without these defenses, it would dissolve. It needs your inadequacy to keep the attack and self-attack in place. It sets up a vicious circle to ensure its safety at the expense of yours. Attack and the inadequacy it generates are destructive to you and your relationships, setting up endless troubles that keep you from joining and having happiness.

It is equality that allows joining. It is joining that brings happiness and transcendence. If you have been favoring attack, or believing in the smallness about yourself that justifies attack, you have been working against your own best interest. When you do not feel adequate, rather than attack you could either commit to equality until you experience the mutuality that doesn't allow attack, or you could sit quietly and ask Heaven, "What is my value?" The words that come in will bring back your value and confidence.

Do not choose weakness when love and fullness are possible. Your ego is the principle of separation. It is your self-concepts that wall off the world. This includes Heaven and your partner. If you are willing to give up on the altar of pain the identity you made for yourself, you could have more of your real Self and fewer walls and illusions. This Self has more power and love and it extends instead of attacks.

Commit to yourself. Extend yourself to know your love and your power. Commit to your partner. Commit to your life and your work. This builds your confidence and your relatedness, dissolving the pain, fear and smallness of the ego.

Chapter 20

Every Emotion Shows a Conflict

Every emotion shows a conflict. Whenever any emotion comes up and there is an upset of any kind, it shows a place in which you have two parts of your mind in opposition. It means you have two different beliefs that are not integrated. If they were, the false elements would fall away and there would be a whole that would bring both a new integrity and greater confidence.

The negative feelings are what keep the parts of your mind separate. They can be slight distractions or major emotional obstructions, depending on how far apart these aspects of your mind are in their beliefs. When the parts come together in healing and a greater wholeness, those particular emotions disappear into peace. When bad feelings come up, your first temptation is to react and put the responsibility for these emotions on someone else. Then you blame and attack, upsetting yourself and removing yourself from peace.

Once an upset surfaces, it is important to commit to healing. If you realize that healing is what you are here for, that it is your purpose in life and your purpose in the world, you would know all good things come from reaching greater peace and wholeness.

You will forget this important principle many times until you make it a part of you. Typically, each time a bad feeling arises, you will once again think that someone else has made you feel bad, and make them wrong. If you embrace what comes up as the opportunity to heal, if you commit to your healing, get beyond the belief it is anyone's fault, but experience the gratitude of having this buried conflict shown to you, then what occurs becomes an opportunity for a better way. Otherwise, it becomes a fight, a conflict that is now projected on to someone outside of you. You will make this person wrong by trying to project the guilt on them. But no one needs to feel bad about it, if you are willing to commit to the better way that comes of the healing process.

If you can communicate with the intention of healing and bridging the gap between you and the one you are in conflict with that reflects the gap in your own mind, then the bridge building has begun. But if you lose sight of the healing and start judging them, you lose your healing opportunity. Examine now the conflicts you are in. Commit to **your** healing. Let these next words that come from A Course in Miracles be your mantra: "I could have peace instead of this". Repeat this until you are once again at rest.

Chapter 21

Everything Negative Hides Fear

Everything negative hides fear. This includes emotions and any experience that is not a positive one. Negative situations in the world are made of lots of fearful relationships. Here are the key dynamics that bring fear about: separation, conflict, judgment, attack thoughts and authority conflict. As soon as you separate from someone or something, fear comes up, with all the things that generate fear, such as loss, feelings of inadequacy, abandonment, neediness, scarcity, resistance and having a split mind. You cover over these things with activity, pushing yourself, setting too many goals and expectations of yourself and others. In an 'advanced case' of fear and inadequacy, you attempt to use perfectionism. There is also denial, dissociation and, finally, attachment and fusion to form a level of *faux*-bonding. This looks like love but it is a form of sacrifice that denies equality.

When the split mind occurs as bonding is lost, you want different and opposite things. You want love, happiness and success, but you also want to hide, have an excuse not to shine, be independent and do things your way. The competition within you leads to competition outside of you, generating fear from the competition but also because each 'part' of the mind is frightened it won't get its needs met.

With attack thoughts you see the world sending back to you what you are sending out. You reap what you sow. It is the same with judgment, which is a form of condemnation and attack.

With an authority conflict, you feel threatened by those above and below you. This makes you feel you have to protect yourself from your own attempts to be right, have the final authority, do things your way and be the boss, whether you are right or not. Equality and the bonding that it brings is the natural antidote to this.

One way to heal a negative experience of any kind is to heal the fear that lurks beneath it. To restore bonding by any of the healing principles is the way to remove fear.

Willingness on your part cuts through the fear. Willingness gets you past the paralysis of fear. Even the willingness to be willing is enough because Heaven and your higher mind do the rest. Grace is another key aspect to heal fear, as fear shows that you are relying on yourself, feel alone and lack trust. At one level, all fear comes from the choice to invest in fear and worry, which is also a form of attack, rather than trusting and having faith in God to take care of your every need as His beloved child.

As you learn to reconnect, increase friendship, foster mutuality and choose love and trust over fear, your fear dissolves, increasing the sweet ease in your life. Slowly but surely your forgiveness grows. You overlook what you thought could not be overlooked, and what was seemingly chronically stuck is transformed. You have moved beyond the trap. The fear underneath the problem is no longer trapping you. You win back the life of love and creativity that you were designed for.

Chapter 22

Anger is a Form of Resistance

Anger is trying to change what is through bullying. What is or how things are shows that something is amiss according to your script. Your wishes have been thwarted and there is frustration because things have gotten out of control. Anger is an attempt to correct things and put them back in line with your conscious wishes so it will meet your needs. You are resisting what has occurred and are attempting to put the situation back the way you want by bullying others with your anger. You are resisting the flow. Were you to accept what has occurred that you are resisting, it would be let go of. It would no longer stop you or cause you the pain that led to your anger. You would move forward from a place of upset to one of peace that comes from the acceptance of what is occurring.

Anger shows your resistance to the hidden script you are writing, which conflicts with what you consciously want. What life or others do that seems at odds with what you want fits the hidden script. The extent of your pain has to do with the extent that what you wish for consciously is at odds with a deeper script that you are writing but have hidden from yourself. This deeper script has ego payoffs that include specialness, independence, attack, self-attack and, as a result of what is occurring, taking control and doing things your way. All of this gives you an identity at the cost of pain, which the ego hides and dissociates for you.

The amount of pain you experienced shows just how disparate these two wishes of the ego are. They are opposite belief systems. They want different things. The ego hides its agendas because they are completely at odds with your conscious mind, which wants love and success. The ego wants separation because that is what gives it existence. It wants specialness and self-aggrandizement and, if it cannot have grandiosity, it goes for the specialness that comes of being a victim and suffering. It wants attention but doesn't want to give attention unless it gets something in return. It doesn't know of the benefit and abundance that comes of generosity. It is calculating and wants return on its investments. The ego is not about sharing but about taking. You may have conscious benign belief systems about giving that are at odds with the hidden ego belief systems of separating and taking. The amount of pain in a victim situation, which is a form of attack toward significant people, shows how much anger there is that others did not do what you wanted them to do in the past. All pain shows a desire to take. In the present, unmet needs from the past can show up as revenge. "I'll show them. Now they'll be sorry when I get hurt or lose myself in some way."

If you want your power back, become aware of the hidden script. Forgive yourself, and others that you have used to act out the hidden agenda for yourself. Acknowledge what you sought to get by this hidden script. See it as the bad deal it was and is for you and your happiness. You can use these situations to heal yourself and free others. Integrate the hidden script with your conscious wishes to get a new integrity and wholeness. Integrate this and any ancillary emotions that come up, melting them into your higher mind through integration. This removes these blocks to your higher mind and allows you to regain your wholeness once more, so instead of pain and resistance there is a new confidence.

Chapter 23

Every Emotion Serves a Purpose

Every emotion serves a purpose. It is as if every negative incident you have in your life serves the ego's purpose of stopping you and building itself, while the higher mind's goal is that each emotion be used for healing. Without awareness, the emotion stands as a monument of pain. It becomes the finger on the trigger of accusation and attack. It becomes your symbol of righteousness. The emotion proves you are right and gives you the excuse to do whatever you wanted to do in the first place but didn't fully give yourself for.

It is important to ask yourself as every negative emotion surfaces: What am I using this for? What is the purpose of this? What benefit did I seek to gain? What does this allow me to do? What is it I don't have to do? What is my payoff for this? What excuse does this give me?

When you find your answers, you can choose again. You don't have to keep investing in something you know to be untrue that won't bring you happiness. Happiness comes from joining and your emotions separate you from others, yourself and Heaven. Your emotions were inside all along but it is likely that you weren't aware of them, or certainly not to the extent you are now. Chances are if you haven't gone back to where they began in the past, you are not aware of the full extent of them.

It is quite helpful to determine what you will use an emotion for before you react. If you set up a categorical goal such as healing, then at some point as the emotion occurs, or soon after, you begin to use this emotion, not as a sign of guilt on someone else's part or as a reason to pull back, but as a means to heal and have deeper peace and intimacy.

This means you are either feeling peace or have the means to use something to become more whole, confident and connected.

What will you use this emotion for? To build your life or to build your ego? You have discovered an emotion that was in you all along. It simply needed this incident to trigger the emotion so you could become aware of it. Will you invest in Heaven's plan or your ego's? Will you invest in yourself and the truth, or in being right?

Make enough choices in the same direction and they become an attitude. Decide now how you would use your emotions and commit to that direction. The quality of your life depends on it.

Chapter 24

All Emotions Show Resistance

All emotions show resistance. As such, they are reflections of fear of the next step as well. All emotions also reflect a need that is not being met because the need reflects ambivalence. If you were open to receiving what you need, you would already have received it.

All emotions show a split mind. There are two parts of your mind that are refusing to go forward together until their individual form of being right and getting their needs met is guaranteed. The more opposite these parts are, the more you feel in a dilemma and, at worst, crucified.

It is the integration of these different aspects of the mind that brings peace and the next step. Commitment to the next step also heals the dilemmas and brings integration and partnership. Continued commitment heals unconscious elements and core self-concepts, leading you to vision and new levels of your purpose. It is the desire to give yourself fully to your purpose and God's Plan for you that contains no sacrifice.

The emotions that come up seemingly as a result of the situation were already inside, waiting for a chance to show themselves. You can treat these emotions simply as the next lesson in your soul's personal curriculum because, if you don't treat them as lessons to be learned, you will suffer resistance. It is your choice. The willingness to learn the lesson puts your faith in healing and corrects the bit of faithlessness in yourself, others and Heaven that your resistance shows.

Chapter 25

Stubbornness is a Form of Fear

Stubbornness is a form of fear. You want to be right. You are afraid of being both wrong and having to change. You dig your heels in. There is a feeling of inadequacy under your stubbornness. You don't want to be pushed. You label yourself as 'strong-willed' rather than stubborn.

There are other forms of stubbornness that begin with unwillingness and resistance. It is willingness that heals the fear of these things. But stubbornness can progress to being unamenable, obstinate, 'bloody-minded', implacable, recalcitrant, immovable, obdurate, being ossified and incorrigible. Many times, these are the dynamics under the misery of chronic problems and the tantrums that hide under them. This, in turn, comes from bad attitude, negativity, saying no to life, bad faith, passive aggression and contrariness. You are afraid to give up a certain self-concept you have built. It doesn't matter if this personality seems to be negative or positive. If you made it, you are attached to it and sometimes forcefully resist such change. As a result, you embody the shadow figure or the self-concept of the 'dinosaur'.

The shadow is a split in your mind that you judge, split off, repress and many times project, but always attack yourself for. A self-concept doesn't carry the amount of guilt and self-hatred of a shadow figure. You think a self-concept is normal even though others around you may notice and even strongly object to your being so stuck in your ways.

Change and learning keep you young. Commitment to the next step, your partner and your relationship as the central part of your life, keeps you changing and growing. A relationship is like a workshop that promotes healing and transformation. Like a workshop, a relationship is an investment in yourself, your growth and your happiness. This comes about through ever greater relatedness and bonding, which is a deepening of intimacy in the relationship, and greater success outside the relationship for you both.

You may be decades into your marriage before you reach such stubbornness in yourself or your partner because the roots of the stubbornness and rebellion that are present within us are usually locked away in the unconscious. Your partner may actually surrender and be very flexible until you reach this deep level or a chronic issue. To get beyond this stuck place creates more happiness, love and bonding, or it can be the rocks your life and relationship founders on. If it shows up in the power struggle stage of a relationship, it shows that you and your partner are more wounded and have more healing work set up for yourselves. If you add up **your** stubbornness and that of everyone around you, it equals all of your stubbornness that is present at conscious, subconscious and unconscious levels of the mind.

Commit to learning and change. If you are stuck in some way, you are both stubborn and wrong about something. Ask for the truth and blessed change to regain your freedom.

Chapter 26

Your Expectations and Demands Can't Get Satisfied

Your expectations and demands can't get satisfied. Your expectations may be met because of your demands but this is almost always done under duress. The sacrifice part of meeting someone's demands is not a true giving and so doesn't meet the need or satisfy the craving.

Also, demands are a form of taking that satisfies the ego but not you. The ego only values what it takes but taking doesn't meet the need, because if the need were met, bonding would occur once more. As a result, part of the ego would be lost as it is the principle of separation and the opposite of bonding.

When a need occurs, it does so because of the choice to separate, go independent and invest in the ego. Consciously, you want your need met. You want the love and success bonding brings. Subconsciously, you are afraid to lose your independence and resist the very things you might be working hard for.

In every expectation there is a picture about how things should be. If it doesn't fit your picture, or even if it does, you are not satisfied and come up with another fantasy of what would satisfy you. This easily puts you on a treadmill that never gets to the end. Paradoxically, as you let go of your pictures, you feel satisfied with what you have. As you let go of your attachments, you can finally be fulfilled. Being empty-handed allows you to be fulfilled.

Chapter 27

Your Problems Show You are Blaming Someone

Your problem shows you are blaming someone. This is a type of subconscious attack, hidden by the fact that it looks like a place where you were injured. Yet, this setback hides your blame of someone. "Look at what you did to me," the problem yells out at some significant person and society in general. It is also a place you accuse God of doing such a thing to you. Subconsciously, you take no responsibility for what is happening in your life and it is this, as well as blame, that dissociates your power. Your mind is at odds with itself when you suffer a setback of any kind.

When you have setbacks, it is helpful to ask yourself who you are blaming. Look at what you are willing to suffer to make this case against another.

Of course, blame **hides your own guilt**. And guilt always sets up self-punishment. Attack and self-attack are a vicious circle. You cannot attack another and not attack yourself. Conversely, you cannot attack yourself and not attack those around you and those you love.

Take a look at your life at the present time. Where are there setbacks and who are you blaming? Then go back through your life and examine your major setbacks and the blame under them. Who was the blame toward and about what? Then go deeper and see what you were blaming yourself for. Finally, ask yourself what you were blaming God for.

If you begin forgiving whoever you blamed, including yourself and God, you will find that your perception of the incident changes. Once you forgive enough, then the whole story of what occurred changes in a significantly happy way. You can get your life and your power back in this way.

Chapter 28

When You Experience a Loss, Similar Unfinished Mourning Comes Up for Release

When you experience a loss, similar unfinished mourning comes up for release. When there is someone or something you cannot seem to get over, your holding on may be fed by similar past losses.

Once, in 1975, as I was mourning the end of a relationship with a girlfriend, I walked through my cottage feeling the emotion in order to release it. After about 45 minutes I had a 'flashback' of being about two years old, standing in my crib crying for someone to come and pick me up. When the emotion of this scene released, my letting go took a marked turn upward. I have had similar break-ups with girlfriends that led to releasing what was still being held onto from previous relationships, and other places in my childhood.

When you do not let go of what is lost, it becomes depression. But what is let go of opens the way for a new beginning. If you realize that an unmourned loss sets up a pattern of loss, you will be more motivated to let go. Sometimes depression is used as a defense against future loss because if you are unwilling to let go and engage, you believe it will protect you from further loss. It's a poor strategy as depression locks you into the very feeling of loss that you are defending against. You stay in the emotion of loss to prevent loss, proving once again that defenses lead to what they are defending against. This kind of subconscious, bad ego logic is quickly released once it is brought to light.

If you went beyond all subconscious and unconscious loss in your letting go, you would eventually get back to the primordial sense of loss that took place in the Fall – your separation from Heaven into the dimension of separation and time. The purpose of time is to restore what you lost through bonding and to bring about the forgiveness of grievances that come from loss so you are restored to Oneness. The purpose of time is also to let go of the idols, attachments and fantasy that hide loss, as well as the split mind that keeps loss ongoing.

When you fully let go, something much better comes to take the place of what was lost. Do you have the courage to have it get better? Do you have the courage to reach a new and better place in your life? All pain comes from attachment, which is counterfeit bonding. Look for your attachments and, by letting them go, recover lost bonding and save yourself future pain.

Chapter 29

Receive Your Inheritance

Receive your inheritance. It has been given to you. You have been given the deed to the Universe. You are the child of All That Is. You are a spiritual prince or princess, but over the eons you have turned yourself into a slave, giving up your power and hiding your identity as spirit. The separation that is your ego causes you to turn away from yourself as limitless light, a child of God. You have a rich Father. Your older brothers and sisters were all saviors of humanity, but you are frightened of your power and the freedom within you that is possible. Even now, in every problem you experience, Heaven extends gifts, grace and miracles to you as the solution.

Grace, which is God's Love for you, pours down on you at every moment. He is giving you everything by His very nature but you are receiving so little. This is because you want to at least *appear* to do it all yourself. This is because you don't want to acknowledge that you have a Creator but you want to think of yourself as self-made. But a prince or princess has a lineage and your acknowledgment is your gratitude for what has been given you. Your gratitude is shown by how much you share those things that have been given to you.

Heaven is giving you everything but you receive so very little. Allow yourself to receive the next giant gift that Heaven has for you. Open the door to it. It will take you to a new level of love and happiness. It will show as a new level of spiritual awareness and giftedness. Each of you has been given this heritage. So few of you embrace it. You can embrace it now. A spiritual prince or princess inspires by their love, beauty and grace. It is their *being* rather than their *doing* that makes all the difference and you could help so many people by the choice to embrace your spiritual heritage. Your destiny is who you came to be. This spiritual prince or princess is who you came to be. Bless the world and bless your life by no longer hiding and running from your destiny.

Chapter 30

Course Corrections are Needed

Course corrections are needed. An airplane flying from one destination to another does not fly straight to its destination. Along the way, the flight engineer takes note of the plane's position and corrects its flight path numerous times. It is the same in life and relationships; you need many course corrections. That is what learning is for: to correct your course.

The first thing is to keep examining your relationship to yourself, to your partner and family, your work and your life. If you don't have the awareness that something needs correction, you don't try to fix it. It is natural to correct something when you know it is off-base. In regard to yourself, examine yourself physically, emotionally, mentally and spiritually. It is helpful to spend some time reflecting on each category and what is missing in it and what you could do to correct it. You don't have to figure it all out. The answer is already inside you. To find the answer you simply need to relax enough for the answer to come to you. Your job is to *want* the answer with all your heart. To commit to it time and again brings you ever closer, until the answer is clear. The answer carries both the energy to bring about the correction and the motivation to have the answer realized. Don't believe the ego's voice telling you it is too hard or impossible to change. It is never Heaven's Will for you to be stuck, so there must be a way through. Your job is the willingness. It is Heaven's job to bring it about.

One key element to examine as you reflect on corrections is your heart and the quality of your life. Are there fights that speak of hidden fear and guilt? Do you feel deadness in any part of your life? If so, you need to get your heart fully operational. The deadness is primarily a defense that is used to cover your fear of partnership, success, intimacy, your purpose, your self, etc. You can get over the fear through forgiveness, giving yourself fully in whatever you do, including yourself, and listening to the inspiration that wants to come to you.

Next, examine the happiness quotient in your life. If you don't have much happiness, you are off-course on many levels. Happiness is a by-product of love and giving yourself passionately. Happiness depends on the amount you give and let yourself receive. This is the opposite of the ego, which doesn't value anything unless it takes it. This comes from separation and leads to manipulation, power struggle, hurt and withdrawal. Taking closes you down so you don't appreciate what you take, what you have or yourself for that matter. Giving opens you so you can enjoy and receive. It creates flow and brings happiness. Take a look at your life. It is the result of all the decisions you have made at conscious, subconscious and unconscious levels. Decisions made at significant moments became patterns in your life for better or worse. Keep making similar decisions and they become an attitude. This is your direction. Decide for life.

You may not be aware of the many decisions that have led you to being in the position you're in, but that is because you have only a relatively small part of your mind that is conscious. The rest is kept below the level of awareness but you can bring it back to conscious awareness through choice, desire and intuition. Take responsibility for your life and your problems or you will never be able to change them. Keep choosing to correct your course or you will forever be blaming others for where you are off course. It is time to bring back the joy and zest to your life and you can only do this if you periodically check on how you are doing.

Chapter 31

Criticism is Arrogant and Competitive

Criticism is arrogant and competitive. There is no centered place that criticism comes from. What is helpful is a sharing of discernment and instruction. The rest establishes superiority and speaks more of the criticizer than the one criticized. Criticism is the attempt to correct another and that is the arrogant part. It is arrogant to disregard that what you perceive is projection, and that you are responsible for what you see and experience. This is because your experience and perception come from choices made from amid the collection of beliefs you have about yourself. Your criticism is an attempt to distance yourself from what you have judged in yourself and another so as to show that you are better than what you have criticized.

Criticism as competition leads to power struggle or deadness as you withdraw from the fight or competition. Both arrogance, which is an attempt to compensate for feeling small and inferior, and competition side with separation and the ego's attempt to build your specialness while putting another down. For a successful relationship, it is important to let these go as mistakes, be aware of collusion in regard to what you experience in another, and help instead of judge.

Chapter 32

Anger Attempts to Place Your Responsibility on Others

Anger attempts to place your responsibility on others. When you are angry, you are declaring that what occurred went against your wishes and that life or another was wrong to act that way. You deny that what occurred has to do with transference, a pattern from your past that you brought into the present, to this particular here and now, because it served some purpose for you. You also deny that this event was part of a script you wrote, again for some particular reason, as well serving as an opportunity to break away and do things your way while attacking another and yourself. Your anger is a form of emotional bullying to control another, either through force or guilt. Anger is not responsive to the emotion that it was meant to defend nor is it responsive to the other but uses them to project on. The self-concepts you have that you don't like are pinned on someone around you, while you pretend it has nothing to do with you and everything to do with them. The world is your mirror, and all your anger attacks you as well as the other.

Look deeper. Take responsibility. Heal on the many layers available to you. Don't be a bully. Your anger is a form of control. Given all the dynamics stated above, righteous anger is not right but a defense against hidden guilt. Your righteousness misses a chance for healing that could make a big difference in your life.

Chapter 33

All Emotions Signal Fear and Guilt

All emotions signal fear and guilt. Emotions come from the space where splits occur, and are maintained by the separation. Fear and guilt are two of the main emotions that come up besides whatever other emotion you are experiencing. If you feel anger, you are also afraid. If you feel hurt, you feel guilt and so on and so on. When you have an emotion, you are not only afraid of the future, you are stuck in the past. You are afraid the future will be like the painful past when you lost bonding. Guilt, which you use to attempt to protect yourself from what you are afraid of, actually programs you to be afraid. Fear attracts what it is afraid of and guilt sets up punishment in an attempt to pay off your guilt. Your fear and guilt tend to remake the emotions of painful events, setting up self-defeating patterns. You may suppress, repress or compensate for these emotions but they are still within, drawing to you what you dread. Only by letting go of all the emotion will a renewed bonding generate more confidence and a new beginning. Fear and guilt set up a vicious circle of guilt from the past and fear of the future, keeping you from love in the here and now. Don't invest in the illusions of these emotions. Ask what you are using them for and, when you see the mistake of these choices, let them go. Choose love instead. You deserve it.

Chapter 34

Emotions and Greed Go Together

When you are connected, the mind is whole. You have one goal and there is a natural flow toward it. There is no need for hard work. Much is accomplished but it is easy. You can receive. When emotions come up, it is from bonding already lost in the past and compounded now in the present. The hidden dynamic present in all pain is that when it comes up you are choosing to break bonding because you think you would be better off on your own. This is completely repressed in victim situations, but a victim situation speaks of your willingness to play a victim role in order to be independent. You fail to realize that this hidden independence is also a role and you cannot really receive for it or enjoy it. This leads to indulgence. What always comes along with victim and independent roles is the sacrifice role, and the sacrifice role is multiplied because it is also used to pay off the guilt of indulgence. Roles lead to deadness and loss of heart. Since you can't receive, you want more and more but can't be satisfied. Thus lost bonding and dissociation feed your greed. You can get and take but not enjoy and so you are caught in the vicious triad of victim-sacrifice-independent roles that keep you in deadness rather than authenticity and partnership.

To use your emotions as the indicator of a mistake you made and to commit to re-bonding heals present pain and the repressed pain that amplified it. It also heals the insatiable emptiness that wants to swallow the world.

Chapter 35

Emotions Have a Pay-off

Emotions are meant to reach a certain goal. They are an attempt to have a pay-off. Emotions are purposeful, as is everything that you do or experience. It all serves you in some way. There is something you are trying to get by it, something you are using as an excuse, something you are trying to protect, some old guilt you are trying to expiate, and some messages you are passing to significant people. You are complaining, declaring an injustice, cutting yourself off from others, yourself and Heaven. You are taking a step away from life. You are making a mistake and using emotional blackmail to control. You are calling for help and for love. You are trying to get attention and be special. You are trying to hide and giving yourself an allowance for something you always wanted to do, or an excuse not to do something you didn't want to do. You place yourself in a victim position and have taken up sacrifice. You are trying to be right and trying to prove your point, both at the same time. You are turning away from a soul gift, Heaven's grace, your purpose and destiny. You are refusing to step up. You are hiding and playing small. You are breaking bonding and adding another self-concept to the shell of personality. You are increasing your fear and guilt, while you are attacking, framing the one who you promised to help, and going for revenge. You are siding with the ego and rebelling against Heaven. You are adding to your stubbornness and fear of change and you are increasing your self-consciousness, busyness and stress. You have split your mind and added dissociation to lessen the wound. But you are hiding what needs healing. You have turned away from the light. You are doing all of this and more at the same time.

It's time to be aware of what you are up to that you usually hide from yourself, so you can make more informed choices and generally heal yourself, knowing there must be a better way. All of this is what you have relegated to your subconscious mind, but you can only find what you have hidden by strong intention and knowing that it is there. When you have discovered the truth about an incident that led to your emotions, you know that no one is to blame but everyone is responsible. You can use your responsibility to free everyone.

Chapter 36

Your Self-Attack Attacks You

Your self-attack is not only a disregard of yourself, it is a kind of spite because you don't value yourself. Yet, the spite is also against your Self. You are siding with your ego against your spirit. Siding with separation is an attempt to keep a certain *status quo* in your life. This fear of going forward may last a while but sooner or later life smashes against your complacency. Many times this blindsides you because you stopped and blocked the very source that would bring grace and miracles. Its purpose is to free you from where you were stuck.

Chronic guilt, and its incumbent self-punishment, is your way of blocking Oneness and staying separate. Hurting yourself, much in the way a petulant child will hurt themselves to express anger at parents, is your attack on Heaven. Yet, Heaven looks with trust and compassion, knowing that at some point you will realize your mistake and move forward again in a way that brings you closer to Spirit, your true Self.

Chapter 37

Problems Show a Lack of Emotional Integrity

Problems show a lack of emotional integrity because a problem comes from your split mind. Your split mind reflects a loss of integration. You want two or more different goals to occur, some of which are completely different. Consciously, you want love but you hide in the subconscious the side you identify with least. Then, you project it out as some outside obstacle.

If you only wanted one thing, it would naturally be yours quickly and easily. This is the nature of the mind. But when the mind is split, it can literally go off in dozens of directions, all of which can neutralize the movement forward to success.

When you have a problem, the split mind that began with a separation on our part contains many painful feelings. There is always loss, hurt, fear, guilt, loneliness, and feelings of weakness, inadequacy and blame, to name some of them. You have projected out that someone did something to you that caused you to separate. You hide from yourself that you sided with separateness, invested in the ego and used this to break bonding. You hide from yourself that you did all this to be independent.

The ego reassures you it will take care of the pain and it does this through dissociation. This doesn't take care of the problem; it covers it over. The pain is still within you; you are simply unaware of it. The law of attraction works to draw similar pain to you, which comes toward you, triggering the old pain. This can cause trauma but it is important to know that the pain you are feeling was already inside you. When this comes to the surface, the ego wants to compound the pain while your higher mind wants to resolve it, going all the way back to the root of the separation that opened when the pain appeared. Will you choose to heal or will you choose to compound the pain?

There are levels of lack of integrity that go even deeper. You deny the emotions that are present in the problem. This denial is a defense and it is an attempt to protect separateness. You want the solution to the problem and you don't want it because it serves where you have identified with your ego.

Another equally true way of saying this is that you chose the problem. This was to protect your fear, cover your feelings of inadequacy, pay off guilt, attack others and yourself, gain control of others and yourself, maintain a grievance so you have control over others or yourself, run from your purpose and many other reasons. Naturally, you hide all of this from yourself and simply feel you have a problem.

If you realize that you are responsible for the problem, and are willing to forgive yourself and everyone else in the situation as many times as necessary to completely shift your experience and dissolve the problem, you will free and empower yourself.

Chapter 38

Your Problems Show You a Place of Contraction

Your problems show you a place of contraction where you chose smallness over your giftedness. Each problem shows a split in your mind and each split in the mind shows a place of lost bonding. Your lost bonding was caused by your choice, either at a conscious and repressed or at a subconscious level. Even your trauma was a part of your Smallness Conspiracy. It was your desire to hide and to run from your purpose that caused the split from bonding. As a result, you built self-concepts and what was a smooth and easy way became a struggle caused by the conflict of a split mind. When you avoid your purpose, you avoid your greatness and the door of transcendence. The desire to hide that comes from the ego, is at war with your yearning for your higher Self, for knowledge of your limitless spirit, and for Oneness.

When you contract, you shrink a couple of sizes. This serves the ego. Some people who are over-inflated are merely compensating for their sense of smallness. You live in a world of smallness. People are afraid to be who they came to be. There is still a mass exodus away from our purpose and destiny. Born into a world of pygmies, you are afraid to show your true stature as a giant.

Your commitment to your purpose is commitment to your greatness. Your commitment to your destiny is commitment to your mastery. This is the truth as it shows itself in the mind. It is the truth to embrace your purpose and destiny. It is the truth to recognize yourself as a Child of God and embrace your enlightenment. This is what you came for.

You came to run the race. You did not come to shuffle backwards. It is easy to settle and adjust to your world but you came to help as a leader and a friend. You came to bless the world by your vision. You came to bridge Heaven and earth by your mastery. You came to know Oneness through the pathway of enlightenment and the higher regions of consciousness.

Today, commit to your greatness. Do this again and again. Visionaries radically open themselves, willing to venture it all, and then give themselves greatly. What is it that you want for your life? Is your hiding justified? Do you want more for yourself? Do you want more from life? If you do, then you must give yourself completely.

Chapter 39

If You Lose Heart

If you lose heart, you lose the part of your life that makes life worth living. It is your heart that is the key to love of others and yourself. It is your heart that is the key to enjoyment and the ability to receive. If you lose heart, you become dismayed, disheartened, weary, exhausted and, finally, depressed. If you lose heart, you have lost yourself. It is your heart that brings partnership and happy unfolding.

You need to know that losing your heart does not affect just you alone. It affects all those you love and those close to you. The way you get your heart back once you have been daunted or defeated is:

1. To want it back with all your heart.

2. To place your weary and wounded heart in the Hands of God.

3. To share love with those you love or those who need you.

4. To find what inspires you because it will open your heart.

5. To commit to having all of your heart back.

6. To know you came to heal the place you are stuck. It hides greater success and love. Commit to your next chapter.

7. Take full responsibility and turn your trap over to Heaven's Trading Post. There is a good deal on traps today.

8. Choose someone you love and keep joining them step by step through whatever experience is in the way.

9. Ask for a miracle. Everything you ask for has already been given. Receive the miracle as you ask for it.

Chapter 40

Self-Love is the Key to a Happy Life

Self-love is the key to a happy life. Every time you choose to love yourself, you invite all the good things of life to you. On the other hand, every problem or illness represents a lack of self-love on your part. Self-attack is the biggest problem in the world, constantly breeding attack on others and even more self-attack.

Self-love blesses you while self-attack curses you. Every time you choose self-love, you heal something from the past that would have assailed you as a problem. When you give to yourself, you have so much more to give to life. When you love yourself, you have so much more to give those you love.

When you are stuck in lack of self-love, you can invite Divine Presence to be with you with its immeasurable Love and inestimable value. The boundless Love it has for you will always increase your level of self-love.

Chapter 41

Inflation and Deflation Come from Traumas

Inflation of yourself and deflation of yourself come from traumas. These are two opposite defenses for the same problem. You deflate yourself, thinking that if you deflect attention you won't get hurt again. Or you inflate yourself in an attempt to make up for the loss that you experienced with the trauma. You either deflate or inflate yourself when there is an absence of self-love.

Usually in a relationship, inflated and deflated personalities partner with each other. As a couple progresses, they hopefully become not only more balanced but more equal. If this doesn't occur, then competition can come to the foreground and raise all manner of issues. One person will be the top dog and the other becomes the underdog. The underdog is dependent on the top dog's inflated sense of self. They use it to make up for their lack of self-esteem, but the underdog also experiences resentment about the top banana giving themselves a high place, which seems natural to them.

Commitment to equality and balance is the key here because both top dog and underdog are two sides of the same coin. Each partner rejected the inflation or deflation as dangerous in the situation they were growing up in. Yet, each contains the other in the subconscious. Commitment to balance integrates these splits time and again. It is only when these have been completely integrated that smoothness emerges in the relationship. Only then do the complaints, backbiting, sabotage and resentment fall away because the subtle levels of competition are no longer used in order to hold a partner back.

Let no level of hidden competition hold you back from all the sweet and transcendent intimacy that is possible between you and your partner and you and your family.

Chapter 42

Acknowledging Your Mistakes Begins to Change Them

Acknowledging your mistakes begins to change them. As soon as you acknowledge a mistake, your higher mind kicks in to reverse the damage of the mistake. In this way your mistakes are corrected. You are inspired to see a better way and the trap unravels, leaving you with the lesson learned, a step forward in life and greater confidence.

An emotion lets you know that you have made a mistake. If you acknowledge that it is a mistake, rather than using it to feel righteous and justified in bullying or emotional blackmail, then it can be corrected. Your righteousness and your feeling justified in an emotion ignore the fact that at a deeper level of the mind you choose that emotion and what brought it about for a certain reason. As A *Course in Miracles* states: "You are not upset for the reason you think." Your righteousness hides feelings of guilt. It denies the part you played in the emotion at subconscious and unconscious levels. Once you acknowledge that you have made a mistake, you begin to learn the lessons involved. This shows a willingness to go forward that makes healing an emotion an easy and natural task. The way becomes smooth and your maturity and emotional integrity grow.

Chapter 43

Love is Beauty

Love is beauty. The love that you have for one another creates beauty in and around you. Beauty is typically aesthetic fineness of form. But there is another beauty that emanates from the heart, blessing all who behold it with openness, and who then respond with heart blessings of their own. Love brings a beauty that adds to the cache of beauty, which at the deepest level binds the world in Oneness. Love is what reminds you of the Heaven that you are evolving toward. It is a place of love and light. It is the love that you have for anything that allows it to become beautiful. This blossoming into beauty is a fragrance that touches everyone around you.

The love you have within makes you beautiful. Love has the ability to open others and beauty has the same effect. Love creates, while beauty is created. Beauty is the effect of love.

Love is giving, extending yourself, sharing and receiving. The more love you express, the more beauty you create. You have the ability to create a Beautiful Life Story for yourself by the love that you give. When you give love in unexpected places, life opens to you. When you give love where there was separation or grievance, healing is created. Love can increase bonding so that the mind opens in joy, and intelligence increases. Love does not demand. It shares itself and blesses what it touches. At the level of *being*, love and beauty are a radiance. It is just what they are; there is no doing. Love simply is and where it is beauty abides.

Chapter 44

Your Experience Emotionally Depends on How You are Using an Event

How you experience things emotionally depends on how you are using an event. If you are using it for healing then, in spite of any suffering or hardship, there is a curiosity about what is really going on and an anticipation about the gifts that are hiding under the pain.

Most people do not know what emotion is truly for, and so the ego hijacks an emotional event and holds you hostage to the pain. But, in truth, an event will either be used in service of the ego or the higher mind. The ego offers you blandishments that cannot possibly make you happy. What it gives separates you from yourself, those you love and life. If you follow the ego, you do not follow the path of happiness. If you follow the higher mind, you neither run from emotion nor do you revel in it with guilt or self-pity. You understand that to go through the emotion as quickly as possible, trusting the process, brings you to a new birth and so you have more of your heart back as a result. The higher mind uses an event for learning and to make you whole again. It uses every emotional event as a way for you to step up, realize your power, achieve more peace and embrace the gifts, purpose and destiny that would transform the situation.

The ego uses an emotional event to get its needs met and gain attention. Yet, whatever you do get, you don't feel satisfied because you feel you have to strategize, albeit subconsciously, to get it. This way does not allow you to receive, only to **get**, which doesn't fulfill your needs. It only makes you hungrier. Getting is the ego's solution to having needs met while still staying independent. The only thing that works for fulfillment is giving or receiving as this restores the bonding.

So, when emotions come up, give them to your higher mind and let it be in charge of them. Then, upset will be used in the service of healing and for that which builds your life.

Chapter 45

Attack is Not Discrete

"Attack is not discrete" is a quote from A Course in Miracles. When I first read it I realized it was so psychologically astute, so accurate and profound that I was inspired. My own work over the decades confirmed this principle and I could see how true it was. Attack one person and it is not a pistol you fire at someone, but a machine gun you take to the crowd. Attack yourself and it has the same effect. It attacks those around you and those you love.

You cannot be angry at one person and not have your attack affect those you love. This includes passive aggression, withdrawal and victimization. It may be aimed at one person but it hits everyone. Everything is connected and so is everyone. You cannot act aggressively with impunity. It attacks you as well as everyone else. I have been able to motivate people to give up self-attack when they saw the effect on their children. Similarly, I have been able to show that a person's anger toward another was having a deleterious effect on their partner. Emotionally, there is a unified field; our emotions affect everyone and this shows directly with regard to anger and attack.

It is time to give up all attack and grievances. As A Course in Miracles states: "You never crucify yourself alone." As you try to nail someone to the cross, you put the hands of the people you love the most over the hand of the person you have the grievance with. It is the same if you crucify yourself; you nail those you love. Do you really want to do this? Attack must be given up completely for you to be free. Now is the time to choose to let it all go. This may be one of the most important decisions of your life.

Chapter 46

Why the Chip on Your Shoulder?

You think there are many reasons to fight but in truth the only good one is to protect yourself. If you let someone injure you it increases your guilt and their guilt also. It can set up a vicious circle of guilt, attack and being attacked. So, if someone attacks you physically it is important to defend yourself rather than sacrifice yourself out of guilt. But other than that, defense leads to attack and sets up another vicious circle of attack.

The first and biggest reason that you fight is that someone is not meeting your needs and you think that they should. They are your partner, your parents, your teachers, your child. This goes on and on and it is the biggest mistake in life and relationships – that you believe someone is responsible for your happiness. You are born in a culture of looking outside yourself. You demand that other people make you happy and you complain or have tantrums to show people just how unhappy you are. *Any problem* is a complaint leveled toward another that they didn't meet your need. A major problem is itself a tantrum that someone didn't do it the way you wanted them to in order to meet your need, which you think is obviously their job and why they were put on this earth. So, if they'd only get with the program, you wouldn't have this problem. What **are** they waiting for?

In speaking of attack in this chapter, I have shared principles of the subconscious mind as well as principles of emotional maturity to bring understanding. Used together they bring success in life and relationships. Any emotion you have is both an upset and complaint that someone didn't meet your need. Emotions are distinguished from feelings that are typically good unless otherwise stated. As you mature you make fewer and fewer demands that your happiness should come from what you feel others need to do for you. Happiness comes from within as you generously extend to life and the world around you. There is a paradox in regard to what you need. What you feel you need is what you are called to give. This is a principle that is very hard to understand for those who still want to 'get'. I have heard numerous men tell me that this principle can't be right because they would give their wives or girlfriends sex "any time, any place or anywhere" and somehow their partner is not forthcoming, so to speak. What they don't understand is that giving sex is not just 'pipe-fitting'. It's about the giving of both intimacy and sexual energy to set the mood. Give intimate and sexual energy like that and it might turn out to be "anytime, any place and anywhere".

Your needs set up most of the fights you have and most of the fights in the world. You both resent others for not meeting your needs and resent them if they do. In the first instance they are depriving you and you feel justified in attacking them for not giving 'what belongs to you.' And in the second instance, where they meet your needs, it comes down to "Just who do you think you are, Mr. or Ms. High and Mighty, taking care of me as if you are God Almighty?" You feel resentful of wanting and being needy. "I could have done it all myself if I just had a little more time." A need is very difficult to fulfill as it comes from a split mind. You want your needs met on one hand and on the other you are pushing people away because if you receive, you would bond again and the hidden part of your mind really wants to remain independent. Your ego's strategy is to **get** your needs met or **take** what you need instead of receiving because then you can remain independent and pretend **you** did it. But the behavior of getting and taking leads to others moving away from you or rejecting your taking behavior. Pain of any sort shows that you were following your ego's idea of surreptitiously trying to get or take.

The second favorite reason you fight is that you want to be right. You don't realize that for truth and peace you need to join and integrate. This allows the best of both sides to come into a new and better whole, both conceptually and energetically. Even if your partner is completely wrong, they have half the energy to help make a new and better whole. Having the best of both sides is what takes you a step forward together. Your ego always wants to be right because it uses righteousness to hide guilt. The more righteous someone is, the more guilt they feel inside. Your ego always wants to make the other feel the guilt. So, you judge, blame, act righteously and project your guilt. Being right is a key aspect of the ego, which it uses to separate and feel superior. This is the very opposite of love. If you've got to be right, you are always itching for a fight. Being right makes you closed, unwilling and crotchety. Your mind is made up and you don't learn and grow. You become a dinosaur and you are hard to get along with.

The third major reason you fight is that you want to win. When you compete you believe that the only way is to win. This makes your partner a loser, which they will certainly resist and resent. Competition leads to fights and power struggles. In competition if you win you lose because if your partner is a loser you pay the bill. When they lose you end up with a less attractive partner. Competition also leads to deadness in a relationship because people withdraw so as not to lose. This is the number one cause of deadness. Only equality works for success. This results in dialogue, sharing and flow.

The fourth major reason you fight is that you want revenge. You have projected out one of your shadow figures on another person. Your ego becomes righteous and closed to love. You use revenge in order to try to assuage all of your losses as well as all the hurts and heartbreak you have not gotten over. Your desire for revenge is almost always subconscious but it leads to havoc as you attack to make up for pain in the past. But revenge does not transform the pain of the past, only healing does that. You want revenge for a past that never was. Your pain shows how much you have hidden from yourself subconsciously. You go on a quest trying to fill needs for every loss and heartbreak that you ever suffered. Pain and need show that the separation, misunderstanding and denial that were part of such previous losses are still intact. Revenge just makes it all worse. As Jesus said, "If you live by the sword, you die by the sword."

A major form of revenge is not just to attack but to get yourself attacked and to make someone else feel bad or guilty about what happened to you. This certainly doesn't work for happiness. Victim-revenge breeds even more loss and heartbreak. What you really hid from yourself about victim-revenge is that you were attacking others not for what they did or didn't do but from what you did or didn't do. Being a victim then is both a form of attack and revenge, as well as self-attack, and all of this is repressed.

The fifth major reason you have a chip on your shoulder is that you are afraid of the next step. You fight because you are afraid of going forward. The fight with the other becomes a good excuse to not step up, change and move on. All of your energy and attention goes into the fight rather than into willingness and saying "yes" to the next step. In a fight, both people are using each other so as not to step forward. All of the energy and attention goes into the fight.

Fighting hides many things from your awareness, such as the fact that your present fights are old fights that you haven't gotten over. Your old fights scripted the whole event, including how the other acted. On the surface you were upset because you felt they were acting in a way you think you didn't want them to act. You were angry or hurt because they broke your rules and didn't follow your script but at a deeper, subconscious level they were exactly following a more hidden script you wrote to give you an excuse to unload your anger, project your guilt, not go forward, etc. Every painful event in your life shows major places in your mind in which you have things buried. If you understood an event fully there would be no one to blame, not even you, and there would be no fights.

Hiding awareness at deeper levels gives you a fight with yourself. Your conscious and subconscious mind are at odds, or sometimes it is two subconscious aspects at odds with each other and your conscious mind. You want two different things. It's like one leg is going in one direction to try to meet a certain need while the other is going in another direction and both want it their way. This leads to much conflict and little success. When you have a fight going on, you do not get much done because you are obsessed and distracted and this adds to your stress.

Most of the people you are fighting with are people that at a soul level you promised you would save from themselves. You can't help them if you judge, attack or withdraw. It is all part of your purpose to help another instead of fight.

This attitude of helping relieves your guilt and sin, emotions and beliefs, hidden under a fight. Helping heals the others of negative emotions while removing the false and terribly destructive concepts of guilt and sin, which you believe unforgivable. This helps all of you. If you were willing to not condemn yourself for what you saw in the other when fighting, then you would both be free and also help the world. So, forgive yourself and play nice.

Underneath any fight there is the fight with yourself. The other in a fight is acting out your unconscious self-concepts and a fight with anyone shows that you are fighting with yourself, with your spirit and it also shows your fight with God, which is hidden in the deepest part of the unconscious. That is because you fear the loss of what you are trying to get from the world. You are literally giving up Heaven on earth and Heaven Itself to go for the baubles and trinkets in the world that you have convinced yourself will make you happy and save you. You give up a world of love for a world of fear. Fighting distracts you from these deeper levels of the mind, which if brought to light would allow you to choose again. Fighting stops you from going forward. You really don't want what the ego promises you will get by fighting. Fighting makes your ego strong and you weak, and it is the weak that attack. Be a lover not a fighter. You will be a lot happier and live a lot longer.

Chapter 47

Emotions are a Form of Being a Victim

When you have an emotion, you are upset. Your emotion states that this experience just happened to you out of the blue and you have no responsibility for it. It states, at least subconsciously, that it is someone else's fault that you are suffering in this way. This is what being a victim is: blaming another for what you are experiencing. Yet, even if your subconscious had not hidden your collusion, your emotions are your responsibility reflecting choices that you made. This includes misinterpreting what the other is doing or what it all means because if you have an emotion, you are misinterpreting. This comes about because you experience pain in seeing others doing what you are doing. You project your patterns onto them. This also includes making them a 'bad guy' because you are using them as an excuse not to face your fear of success, intimacy, your purpose and your destiny. Your judgment, used to hide your guilt, attempts to pin the guilt on another but there is no painful emotion without judgment. So, when you make another a 'bad guy', you experience a great deal of pain to do so.

On the other hand, if your goal was healing, you would use whatever came up not as an obstacle to peace but as a means to peace.

Chapter 48

Emotion Claims There is a 'Bad Guy'

An emotion announces that there is a 'bad guy'. Even seemingly unrelated accidents come from our judgments. Guilt announces the bad guy is us but you also use this guilt to remain truculent and to fight God and Heaven. You are afraid of losing: losing your control, or losing the world you still want to get something from. Look at your life. Is your way what you really want? Wouldn't you rather have the truth?

Hurt, heartbreak and revenge are pretty obvious in their blame. Loss, need and abandonment are a little more subtle but not by much. You blame others, yourself and God for the losses that lead to need and fear. Other emotions that seem to happen 'outside' us, and be caused by events, can be more surreptitious in their blame. It is only when you give up on another and break contact that you feel abandoned no matter what it is they are doing.

Every emotion is tied in with being a victim and our emotions announce, "Look what you did to me!" Even when you are not conscious of it, your subconscious is rife with guilt and blame, which go together in vicious circles. This condemnation sets up a pattern and invites other 'bad guys' to misuse you or gives you the excuse to do it to others. An emotion is thus an attack on another and an attack on yourself.

The key here is not to be dissociated, sterile and defended against emotion but to use every upset as an indicator that you are called to heal, forgive yourself and others, and come to peace. Peace is fertile. It gives rise to creativity, abundance, love and joy. You could choose peace instead of the pain or upset.

Chapter 49

Pain and Emotions are the Price You are Willing to Pay for Separation

Pain and emotions are the price you are willing to pay for separation. Your ego comes from separation. It is an identity you make up from the fractures of separation. The ego is always hungry for separation and the judgments that separate you, placing you above another, or below them, just so long as there is no ego-melting equality.

It may seem that you separate from others because of what they do, but this is our excuse. The predilection for separation was already there because the emotions that come from separation were already inside from past fractures.

To separate or to heal is the choice you have when your emotions appear. Separation has already occurred as evidenced by your emotion but you still get to choose healing or victimization/separation. The goal is not non-feeling but the grandness of peace and the happiness it generates. When separation is occurring, it comes from your choice and this brings with it the pain of emotions. When the choice for healing is made, there is release. Where there is pain in healing, this pain becomes poignant when healing takes place.

On the other hand, when you pull away from another, citing their bad behavior, it means you are willing to suffer. If you were aware, you would see it was your choice to have them act in that fashion *so you could pull away from them*. Your subconscious has a whole other story than the one you have been telling yourself and others. You could have peace instead of the pain of your events. You could join instead of separate. You could help instead of judge. You could communicate and bridge instead of withdraw. You could heal instead of exacerbating the conflicts within you. You could take responsibility instead of being a victim. You could forgive and have peace and friendship instead. You could have accepted the gift within you and the one in them that is waiting to emerge, along with the grace of God's Love that will benefit everyone.

Go back through your life and reflect on when you chose to separate, and make another choice, one that will welcome healing and happiness.

Chapter 50

Loss Comes From Choice

Loss can come because of idle wishes: "I wonder what would happen if... Oh shit!" It can come because of a split mind in which you don't fully value what you lost. Or possibly it is yourself you don't value fully and so cannot fully value another. You could lose something or someone because of the Secret Story in which your loss gave you independence. But, what was the price of all your losses? Bottom line, you lose something because of choice, whether it be because you don't feel worthy of it or you are trying to pay off guilt, are afraid of the next step, are getting revenge on another or you are proving something you are using as part of a power struggle. You see some gain in the loss that you suffer, something that glitters but is not the gold of bonding. Somehow you see some gain in the pain that you are suffering. It serves a purpose for you, such as a need for attention, sympathy or specialness. Healing occurs when you get in touch with what the payoff is, realize that what you thought had value was actually valueless and the position of weakness you thought was strength was utterly mistaken. As a result of your new realization, you are no longer willing to put yourself in a position of suffering. Somehow, you become aware of the illusion you were investing in and, as a result, give it up. You move on beyond the suffering.

At one level, loss is telling you that you have invested in something outside of yourself that you depended on for your needs. When you lost what you were attached to, you suffered. Your loss is life pushing you on to reach a new beginning where you are relying on what is within, so that you share instead of trying to get from something outside you.

Yet, the bottom line regarding loss is the choice you make to lose. This is always to become more independent, and to attack another and yourself. But there is another personal payoff that you thought would produce some gain in your pain. To heal yourself you must realize that whatever you thought the loss would give you is patently untrue. Whatever purpose it served, whatever payoff it was used for, was false and nothing of value could be gained from it when you simply could have had the step forward and learned the lesson the easy way without loss. These losses reflect some of the biggest setbacks of your life. It is now time to see and know what you thought would come out of your loss. What was the payoff you thought you would get by this loss? It was something you considered to be a small price but soon realized was a big one.

See what you chose and be free of your mistaken choice and investment. If the answer doesn't immediately pop into your mind through using your intuition, ask yourself, "What could I have possibly thought to gain from such a loss?" Then hang out with this question until the answer arrives. When it does, it will be obvious it was a mistake and will be totally released if you give up the self-attack the ego will try to use.

Chapter 51

Sacrifice is the Bane of Our Existence

Every time you suffered, you lost bonding. You became emotionally arrested and stuck at that age without awareness or emotional maturity, still caught in the emotions at the time of the wounding. Many of these woundings occurred when you were quite young, even in the womb, and they were used by the ego to build your identity. You sacrifice and work hard to compensate for this young self and for feelings of inadequacy. You sacrifice but you cannot receive for all the hard work. What comes in goes out to pay for the stress of doing and giving without receiving. The hard work of compensation is a defense so there is no real benefit. This is because what comes back in spite of the defense is used to keep the defense intact.

Sacrifice is based on an old judgment that someone didn't take care of you. Yet, it was you who framed them when you could have helped. Since then, you have lived a life of hard labor. The armor of sacrifice exhausts you and blocks the contact that brings success, intimacy and flow. This is as the ego wishes, because going forward begins to melt its walls. Hiding under sacrifice is the dishonesty of the split mind. This comes of blaming another so you could hide. It comes from the unworthiness, guilt and failure that sacrifice is meant to compensate for but in which it never succeeds.

Sacrifice is used for attack. It contains one of the forms of anger, which is withdrawal. You do things for others but you don't give yourself. You keep yourself protected. This sacrifice may lead to burn-out but it successfully hides your fear of moving forward. The ego uses all the forms of sacrifice, such as fusion, co-dependency, and feelings of failure and guilt. These hide your fear and unworthiness in order to keep you from partnership and moving forward. Along with the role of sacrifice there is always the role of neediness or the victim, as well as the role of the rebel, which is really dissociation. This means that, in spite of doing what you want, you can't feel or enjoy and begin to lose heart. These are classic forms of sacrifice, which hide the guilt, which in turn hides the fear. This is all going on subconsciously with sacrifice.

Sacrifice is an emotional trap that keeps you burdened and you use this to avoid intimacy and flow, as well as to deny grace and Heaven. The ego uses sacrifice for dark glamour and getting the attention that comes from you having difficulty. This hides your purpose and destiny from you and pretends there is neither partnership nor Heaven and that you have to do it all yourself. If you see yourself having any of these kinds of thoughts or feelings, your ego has hijacked your life, selling you the idea that independence is the only option. You have set up your life as if this were the only option.

There is a vicious circle of sacrifice, unworthiness, failure and guilt. All roles are sacrifice as they give and do things, but don't venture themselves in the giving nor do they allow you to receive. Sacrifice is inauthentic. It wears masks and armor in a mistaken way in order to keep you safe and make you indispensable. Sacrifice locks you into an untrue past making you think you have to carry the future on your shoulders.

Sacrifice is touted as love but it's a form of self-attack. Anything done through sacrifice could have been done through true giving without sacrifice. It is subconsciously a form of blame, stating that someone neglected you. You used this deception and self-deception as an excuse, a conspiracy against your purpose because of your fear and feelings of inadequacy. Sacrifice is a form of self-pity masquerading as responsibility but it is really a choice to hide and to excuse yourself for not showing up. You are blaming someone who needed your help and your support and now you are imprisoned in a life of sacrifice and unhappiness.

Chapter 52

A Sincere Apology Can Mean a Lot

When you make a mistake, it is important not to defend, justify or give excuses. Simply acknowledging your mistake allows your Higher Mind to begin to correct it. On the other hand, it is also important to apologize to your partner or those around you for mistakes you have made that caused them inconvenience or suffering in any way. An apology does not mean that you are 'bad' or guilty. It does not even mean that you have made a mistake necessarily but that you are sorry that it infringed on another. Even if the mistake was not yours but someone around you was hurt or troubled, a sincere apology has the effect of communicating love and concern, for example: "I'm sorry you are suffering." or "I'm sorry you are having such a bad day." A sincere apology extends understanding, recognition and compassion. It reaches out in tenderness, communicating that you are concerned with how another is faring.

With sincerity, an apology can make a world of difference to those around you. An insincere apology is not in anyone's best interest. Without sincerity, you lose the trust and connection of those you were apologizing to. Apologies build bridges and anything that joins you heals you. So do not misuse apologies because they are expected. Feel the other and their worth and use your words to let your heart reach out in compassion.

Chapter 53

The Pervasive Mistake of Sacrifice

No one but you asks you to sacrifice yourself. Not your family, nor the conditions around you, nor your partner, even if they ostensibly seem to do so. You sacrifice to prove something, typically that you are good or worthy. But sacrifice is a compensation over feelings of guilt and failure that separate you from yourself, others, success and your ability to feel. This stops receiving, enjoyment and flow.

The ego likes sacrifice because it is a defense that keeps the guilt/failure as a building block of the ego. Sacrifice is a shell you build around yourself that constricts and chokes the life out of you as you get older and as the burdens keep growing.

The roles of sacrifice, independence and the victim form an unholy triad that attempts to make up for the loss of bonding but never succeeds. The extent of your sacrifice is the extent of your loneliness, but you try to expunge the loneliness by working harder and staying busy. This doesn't work because when you slow down, there is depression, exhaustion and emptiness. Sacrifice is a way of staying separate and not facing your fear of intimacy, success, or the next step where you believe you won't be able to handle it and fear you would lose independence and control. The role of sacrifice continuously feeds into independence and victim roles. You gradually get tired of being unrewarded and with the deadness and burn-out that sacrifice leads to.

Would you want your child to be in a psychological trap that keeps them from being close to you or from being rewarded for what they give? How much less do you think God would will that for you? God doesn't will sacrifice for any of His children, in spite of what some theologies tell you. How could Love, the Highest Intelligence, want a psychological trap for someone? It doesn't add up. It must be a projection on God. Sacrifice does that. It suggests that you have to sacrifice because of someone else. Hidden inside every sacrifice, there is a grievance about neglect. At some level, you are telling your parents, partner, etc. "This is how you should have done it!" And your sacrifice is that demonstration.

Sacrifice says, "I'll lose now in order to win later." Or, "I'm really the best person. Look how much I'm sacrificing. I'm the morally ascendant one and you are somehow less than that." Sacrifice is competitive, like all roles. Competition leads to fights and generates withdrawal and deadness in relationships and in life.

The price for sacrifice is to have illusion in your life. Sacrifice makes you blind to the lesson that would keep you and those you love from suffering. The message of sacrifice is unrequitedness. "Seek but do not find" is its message. "Work hard but do not receive." Heaven doesn't ask you to sacrifice except to sacrifice the attack where you are crucifying yourself and others. Sacrifice is so pervasive that the confusion of love and sacrifice has been with humanity for millennia. Only when you reach the Union Stage, the very last stage before Oneness, will you divest yourself of this pernicious trap. But as your awareness grows, you will be less likely to sabotage yourself and those you love by sacrifice. If you learn the lesson and give up sacrifice as a way of life, you become the gateway through which those you love and many others will be freed of sacrifice and what is crucifying them.

Chapter 54

Emotions Come From Misinterpretations

Emotions come from misinterpretations. This means that all emotions are illusions that come from an interpretation of what is really going on. It is not what is happening but rather some judgment you have made about what is happening. This means that when any emotion arises, from the slightest irritation to the greatest depression, you are not only off center, you are also off track because of how you are looking at things.

Every emotion screams that someone is guilty because they caused you to feel something you didn't want. This is an interpretation that needs correction; what comes from judgment simply cannot be true. This is when you are called to go within and listen to your own higher mind about how to look at something or someone and what your response should be. A key aspect of living a life of Heaven on earth is to use every emotion as a course correction to get you back on track. If you are dedicated to this, you will transcend all the traps your ego is using to hold you back. You will also catch yourself when you are justifying emotions in areas where you usually don't take a healing attitude, such as at work or in business. And when you know you are innocent, then your ability to help, and let Heaven help those around you, both directly and through you, grows exponentially. When you are innocent, there is no one that your forgiveness would not heal. Use your emotions as indicators of where you need a course correction. It is not your place to judge unless you yourself want to be similarly judged, because you will judge yourself if you judge others. It is your place to correct yourself so you can return to experiencing release and joy.

So, know an emotion is an interpretation that is false. Let this lead to asking within for the guidance to correct the error in your mind. When you are once again feeling peace and responsiveness, you can offer your forgiveness to free those around who helped you find what needed healing within you.

Chapter 55

Emotionally Arrested

Whenever you felt wounded or traumatized, you became emotionally arrested. This creates a problem beside the wound itself because now you have a part that doesn't grow up. Now you have a part of you that is stuck and emotionally immature. For example, you may have a heartbroken three year old and this three year old is sometimes in charge of relationships, success or your purpose. There is no way that this child can succeed. It might have a tantrum, be a tyrant or demand its way but it will end up causing more problems for you.

When someone around you is acting in a less than mature manner, ask yourself how old the wounded self is inside them and love that young self within them. When it receives enough love, it will grow up and melt back into that person, reconnecting wires in their heart, mind and body. In the same way, when you are upset, it means that a part of you is not in the present emotionally but you are acting out something from your past. Ask yourself how old that self is and love it until it integrates. Any major problem or scarcity will have this kind of emotional arrest inside and you can change it to new levels of success quite easily if you recognize it.

Chapter 56

You Only See What You Think You Are

You only see what you think you are. Perception is a mirror, not a fact. What you see in your world shows you what you believe about yourself. When you judge yourself, you split off the judgment, repress it and project it out on the world. You look out and see yourself in the mirror of the world. You chase after things in the world but this is like chasing after what you split off from yourself, pretending you weren't like that and as a result feeling helpless and needy. So, when you attempt to get something, either from someone or from the world, you want it and you don't want it. This ambivalence can cause a lot of striving, until you finally want it enough to have it. Yet, some time after you have it, the self-judgment, guilt and valuelessness that go together lead you to not fully value what you have, and sometimes to lose it as a result.

You see what you think you are. Your self-concepts, which are buried at subconscious and unconscious levels, keep you seeing a world of separation. You see yourself in the ascendant position, morally if in no other way, or below others if you can't be on top. You only see 'the man in the mirror' and if you want to change the world, you must start by changing yourself. This is why forgiveness is so valuable, because while it helps others, it really helps you also. The more you forgive, the friendlier the world becomes. When you turn your judgment over to Heaven, it shows you a way forward for you and the world to be innocent.

It is important that you clean and polish the mirror rather than throw mud or stones at it. To assume responsibility for the world around you gives you back your power and eschews the judgment-guilt that comes of broken bonding.

Today, take responsibility for your life and let your forgiveness flow freely for yourself, others and the world, and you will see a better and better world.

Chapter 57

Emotions as the Absence of God

Emotions show a separation. It is a place you turned away from love into the frozen fields of fear. Emotions show a place you turned away from the light. You forgot God at that moment. God is the Remembrance of love and light. This unifies you where you judge. It brings you back more and more to your essential self on the way to your true Self. As you heal the present emotion that has popped up, you also heal part of the storehouse of past emotion you keep locked in your body as an excuse to be independent, to hide and control. You want to transform your emotions, with all their pain, into feelings that extend from your heart and mind in natural sharing and an overflow of largesse.

When you have an emotion, it is because you are experiencing what you think is an injustice. You don't recognize it as a place where you chose fear instead of love. If you remembered God, Who is always present, you would dissolve the emotion that protests the injustice, which is your excuse to forget God and do things your way. You act as if God did not want what would truly make you happy. Your true will and God's Will are exactly the same. Your ego, the principle of separation, has its own will and it is just interested in building and maintaining itself. It does this through pain and all of its incumbent emotions. God cannot be absent or unjust and be God. He would lose His God license. If you allowed yourself to remember God, you would remember love, beauty and happiness.

You could return to all the places where you suffered in your life and this time remember God and let His Presence dissolve all negativity, dark emotions and the patterns that go with them.

Chapter 58

Greed Exiles Your Heart

Greed exiles your heart. When you are dissociated in an effort to protect your heart, it is actually a trap the ego uses to cut you off from your heart, which is dangerous to the ego. When this occurs, you experience need, independence and deadness. You will either choose to recover your heart through healing the separation that causes the need, or you will choose to follow the ego's lead and attempt to fill the vacuum with acquisitiveness. Greed is based on taking, getting and consuming. Because you have cut off your heart, whatever you get is never enough and, as a result, your greed grows. Whatever you seek doesn't fulfill you, so you seek more of whatever you think will make you happy, such as money, power, sex, fame, food, chocolate, travel, romance.

If you received what you wanted, receiving would satisfy you because, as a form of love, it re-bonds you. When the separation began and you got the three roles of independence, victim and sacrifice, you split your mind. The ego part talked you into paying the price of pain so you could be independent and do things your own way. It does not want us to receive and so speaks of *taking* as the way to stay independent and get your needs met. But the only way to get needs met is to bond. You think that having an independent lifestyle and having things the way you want would make you happy, but while you might have things your way and indulge yourself, you cannot be happy if you have lost your heart. It is your heart that allows you to feel and enjoy.

Greed becomes its own vicious circle. The more you get, the more you want to get and since it doesn't satisfy you, you want more and more and more.

You think you want the control that independence gives you. But it's a bad deal to lose your heart as it is what gives you partnership, creativity, your purpose and lasting meaning in a meaningless world. It is your heart that accesses your will and creativity. Without it, there is no love or joy. Reflect on where you are greedy in your life. What is it that you collect? What is it you can't get enough of? Where are you caught in the desire to consume? Underneath your greed and dissociation is fear and pain, and under that is your solution. This will be some gift that you give instead of something you attempt to take. Turn over your need-greed-defense to be transformed. Ask Heaven's help in undoing this ego prison that you've gotten yourself into with greed and choose love instead. Paradoxically, when you love, you are fulfilled and the fear and acquisitiveness melt away. Choose love when you feel need or greed and watch it begin to dissolve the need in a new flow forward.

Chapter 59

Emotion Expresses Inadequacy

When you experience an emotion, you experience inadequacy to the same extent. An emotion automatically signals that you don't feel that you can handle the situation. An emotion begins at the same time as feelings of inadequacy begin – when you have separated, through some form of judgment or resistance. When bonding is broken with life or another to any extent, you break bonding with yourself. You do not just separate from what is outside but also from what is inside you. This split mind makes you both confident and fearful, both trusting and controlling. This level of conflict hurts your natural confidence to handle a situation. When you disconnect from Heaven and yourself, to the same extent you feel you have to do it yourself but can't. On the other hand, this may have you compensate for your feelings of inadequacy by trying too hard. You are neither self-reliant nor are you allowing yourself to be reliant on Heaven within you, and this doesn't allow for success.

On the other hand, if your first thought in a situation that brings up emotion is one of healing, you will call upon Heaven, or use one of the healing principles, such as forgiveness, to mend what is broken. The wholeness that comes about brings trust and confidence with it and also blesses you and the world around you with a new level of success.

Chapter 60

In a Fight, Ask Yourself What You are Defending

This is an important step in your healing and you can make it a natural part of your transformational backpack. In a fight, you are defending yourself from pain or fear of greater pain. This comes from your past that you still have not healed. These fights need to be healed and let go of so you don't keep generating more situations where there is pain.

You are also attempting to be right, defending a place in which you feel guilty. This calls for self-forgiveness or you will find a 101 ways to punish yourself and others. Innocence is the truth, so let that be your goal. Also, in a fight, you are defending your ego. This is what separates you from the world and is at the root of every problem. Your ego is your authority conflict, which wants to displace God and make itself God. It is time to realize that your ego doesn't love you and is only out for itself. Your higher mind, whose function is to help you heal, is out to help you and everyone. It is your connection to the Tao and the Holy Spirit. Do you want to keep defending what is not true or do you want to build your life? This is an important choice and, if you keep deciding in the same way, it becomes an attitude. Choose for your happiness and you will choose for your higher mind and healing. Your defensiveness is both unattractive and counterproductive. The truth does not need defense, so fighting for the truth is using a process of fear to bring it about. This is obviously an ego strategy to derail the process of coming together with the answer and with another in partnership.

Chapter 61

Forgiveness Brings Peace

When you are upset, you have judged another. That is the cause of your pain no matter what the symptom. But if you forgive that person, as well as yourself and the situation, you are both freer and happier. Sometimes when you have a chronic issue, you need to forgive over and over again. The equation for emotional maturity is simple: if you have upset, it is your upset and your mistake. The subconscious shows this. The present upset was old, unfinished upset and sometimes ancient upset, so the forgiveness must go through layer after layer bringing greater peace. As peace comes about, so does confidence and trust. As complete peace comes about, so does health, love and abundance. Forgiveness is the very essence of healing, the foundation of all other healing principles. As the essential healing principle, when you forgive you become more whole and you not only become more peaceful, the world around you also becomes more unified and peaceful.

Chapter 62

In a Fight, Give up the Temptation to Dissociate

When you fight, you are attempting to break away from the one you are fighting with. It's hard enough dealing with your own feelings when you are fighting but breaking away makes dealing with your opponent's emotions at the same time almost overwhelming. But that's the point that leads to healing. If you didn't dissociate, you would feel how similar your emotions were to those of the person you were fighting with. You would understand them because you would realize you are both feeling the same thing. If your heart were open and you felt what your judgment and attack did to another and to yourself, you would never attack. If your heart were open, attack would be the furthest thing from your mind. If you gave up your dissociation, it would be impossible to attack. You would want love and the happiness that came with it instead.

Dissociation is the ego's solution to the pain that comes about when you separate. Your dissociation leads to denial and you not only cut off feelings and emotions but also what is really going on. You cut off the gifts, purpose and destiny that would totally transform the situation, as well as the lesson you came to learn for greater wholeness. As children and even as adults, your sensitivity makes life seem just too painful at times. But you chose that sensitivity for a reason. You were meant to focus that sensitivity into fine and rare gifts that are deeply responsive. Your sensitivity does not hurt when you have it focused in love, art, healing, and psychic or visionary gifts. Embraced in this way there is natural immunity that builds as your sensitivity is used for its true purpose instead of being used for specialness. The courage that grows allows you to venture with tenderness into intimacy but also into your and others' pain so that healing can take place. When you do this for love or healing, your heart expands. So, ask for the courage to go beyond dissociation. The heart and sensitivity you find within bring partnership and the ability to receive and enjoy. Fine gifts await you when your sensitivity is used in a true way.

Chapter 63

What Constitutes a Fight

Certainly, you recognize a fight when you are attacking or defending yourself but there are many other kinds of fights that aren't as easily recognized, such as when you withdraw or are passively aggressive. Both of these forms are just as aggressive as direct attack. Fighting essentially stops communication. In withdrawal, you believe it is the other attacking you and you are merely protecting yourself, but you are withdrawing rather than responding or helping. And it has the earmark of every fight, which is the fear of the next step and making the other person wrong.

In passive aggression you have denial so you are sometimes quite blind as to how you have been attacking another. Every emotional upset, as well as every victim situation, is a form of passive aggression. This has proved itself consistently in every one of my coaching experiences. I once worked with a woman whose boat had sunk in the ocean and, as she explored her subconscious, she found she was attacking her parents.

You attack out of blame and, before you do this, you attack yourself for guilt that leads you to look for a scapegoat. Any victim situation contains attack and revenge under the pain of your wounding. This goes for illness and injuries, as well as heartbreak or any physical or emotional pain. Also, any scarcity contains attack on your part but again this knowledge is relegated to the subconscious mind.

It is time to become aware of what you have buried in the subconscious. Otherwise, you will go blithely along like everyone else attacking and being attacked, and not realizing how it is holding you up or how it is all a big cover for fear and building the ego when you could be building love, success and abundance.

Chapter 64

Anything Negative that Happens to You is Your Attack

Once again, it is time to venture into the subconscious mind. If you study the subconscious mind, you realize that things don't just happen to you, they happen for a reason. When negative things occur, you are attacking yourself and, under the guise of being a victim, you are attacking someone else. Naturally, you hide this from yourself. You want to think of yourself as an innocent victim and not as an attacker. You want to have a nice, everyday life but you are in denial. You are hiding things from yourself. If you knew what you were really choosing and doing, you would most likely make a choice for something better. The ego is invested in attack and self-attack. This is the very foundation of the ego. The ego tells you that you would die if you went beyond this point, but it is your ego that would die. Whether attack occurs against you or another, it is attack against all. Now it is time to commit to harmlessness, strength and peace, all of which eschew attack. Open yourself to grace and guidance, reminding you to ask for whatever you need, that you might be cherished and given what you need.

Chapter 65

In a Fight, Look for the Past

In a fight, you are always trying to defend yourself against a past in which you were wounded and a past in which you did the wounding. Your fight partner is acting out your subconscious mind: all of the people you grew up with and what you or they did that is unfinished business. And/or you are fighting against ancestral self-concepts passed down through your family, or self-concepts from 'other lifetimes' if you like that metaphor or, if not, ancient, shadow self-concepts within. Ask yourself where this present fight is coming from in terms of your growing up or even from before this life.

Another way to get a sense of where the root of this present fight is coming from is to ask yourself if the root of the fight is old or ancient. If it's old, it's typically from your childhood. If it's ancient, it's coming from influences before this life.

Peace is always being offered from Heaven. In your mind's eye, go to where the root began and ask for Heaven's peace to come through you until that root situation is resolved. You can do this again and again until it is perfectly peaceful there. Then come back to the present fight and channel peace into this situation also.

Chapter 66

In a Fight, Give Up the Desire to Separate

At one level, every fight shows a will to separate. Even if you seem to be fighting to stay together, your subconscious has other plans. This is moving in the wrong direction. A fight calls for attack and brings about illusion, self-attack, fear, denial, pain, dissociation, guilt, unworthiness, feelings of failure, inadequacy, hurt, revenge and possibly compensations to hide these emotions. This is a big price to pay for the illusion of independence. The independence that comes is a role of independence so receiving and enjoyment are blocked. The independent role also brings dependency and victim roles, as well as those of sacrifice and martyr. This blocks flow and partnership, ensures blame, grievance and feelings of both smallness and failure, as well as running from your purpose. Independence dissociates and compensates for these emotions. All of this is going in the wrong direction for love, fulfillment, happiness and success.

Be aware of any desire on your part to separate as it sets up problems and power struggles. Also, be aware that any problem or power struggle in your life comes from the desire to separate. Commit to peace and partnership. Ask for the peace of God. Any joining that occurs will bring peace and healing as well as love, value and joy. This is what you really want. Be vigilant for what you really want.

Chapter 67

In a Fight, Give Up Projections

In every fight there is projection. You project qualities on the other that you have judged, split off and buried. You think you have to defend against these self-concepts that you hate, so you project them and fight against the person you have projected them on. But it is only shadow boxing. You are only fighting what you believe yourself to be. You project your guilt and responsibility onto another and then attack them for their supposed wrongdoings. In your attack you have projected out on them what you need and feel angry that they are not meeting your needs as you believe they were meant to do. It was the judgment about this quality, the splitting it off and projecting it out that made that need seemingly inaccessible to you.

Fights can break out before you even realize that what is going on is your projections on another and these are your disowned self-concepts. But as soon as you are willing to get over your righteous indignation, it is time to realize that it is healing that is called for, not fighting.

One way to end the fight quickly is to pull back your projections. Ask yourself:

What do you see them doing?

What is their problem?

What is wrong with them?

Write these down as they sometimes have a way of slipping your mind once the healing has begun. Pull back the projections one at a time. For instance, if you see them as attacking, check out and see if it is a case of "Oh, yeah, I'm attacking also." This is style Number 1. Or, if you would never, ever attack anyone, no matter what: you would rather die than attack – this is style Number 2 where you are acting in a correct manner but it is a compensation for the attack inside you. Sometimes you have both styles. With either style, you will be torturing yourself about it. Ask yourself how many selves you are torturing within you because of these self-concepts. However many there are, ask yourself if you want to keep doing this or if you want to break these selves out of the torture chamber. In your mind's eye, go over to whoever you are judging and fighting and help them by breaking their selves out of the torture chamber. Imagine yourself helping and possibly embracing the other. Then, once again, appraise them. How do they look to you now? Next, go on to the second quality that is 'their' problem and repeat the process. Do this and it will change your experience of both them and yourself. You and they and the world will be different. You will have peace instead of your fight.

Chapter 68

In a Fight, Look for What You are Trying to Get

There can be no fight unless you are trying to get something. There can be no fight unless both combatants are trying to get a need met from the other. Take a moment and reflect on an attack you made on another. It doesn't matter whether it came from anger or hatred, or whether fear, hurt or guilt drove the attack. Simply reflect on what you were trying to get. Whenever you are trying to get something from someone, you are attempting to stay independent from them. This may work for a little while but usually leads to that person backing away from you.

Fights are primarily about needs. You attack when you feel weak or in scarcity. You want something from the other to empower you or make yourself feel better. Sometimes the attack makes you feel momentarily better. Sometimes the attack even comes from the other wanting to help you but you resent that they are meeting your needs. "Who do you think you are, acting so high and mighty? My attack should put you in your place." Notice that your attack can come whether they try to meet your needs or not.

What you are trying to get from another is typically what you came to give but, in choosing littleness, you decided to hide instead of stepping up and bringing forth this gift that has been waiting in potential. Your sharing of the gift would satisfy you and also open you to receive it from outside yourself. Your giving paradoxically meets your needs and your lack of satisfaction falls away. By sharing the gift, you end the fight.

Examine your fights past and present. Open the door in your mind behind which your gifts have been hidden. Accept the gift and share it. You could also receive a gift Heaven has for both of you and share it. This will end the fight and have you both back in the flow once again.

Chapter 69

How You Fight

Whenever you get angry, feel hurt or guilt, or experience pain of any kind, or if you feel any emotion for that matter, you are in a fight. Essentially, an emotion is a fight. Emotions are distinguished from feelings such as appreciation, gratitude, love or joy. Most of our fights take place below the level of our conscious mind.

An emotion can show itself as a direct attack, such as anger, or as an indirect attack, such as emotional blackmail, for example placing a guilt trip on another. Most people have no awareness of the fighting that takes place at this level but the conflict goes on non-stop. To use an emotion with integrity is to take responsibility for it and use it as an indicator of what needs to be healed within you.

An emotion is a communication that someone has failed you. They failed to meet your needs. This falls under the category of one of the biggest mistakes in life: that others are here to meet your needs. You think they have been assigned to do things your way because your happiness depends on them doing what you want. You get angry when they don't and show it with your emotions. Your emotions let them know when they have done it wrong by you.

When you fight you fight not only with the person you seem to be fighting with, but also with your partner and significant others, such as children, parents, ourselves, your true identity as spirit, and God. A fight thus ranges from your conscious to your unconscious mind.

The body is another area that is used as a battlefield. Health and sexual issues become both weapons and complaints. Besides the people you fight against when you have health or sexual problems, you are also fighting life. To fight life is to attack it or withdraw from it in a death direction.

You feel righteous and justified when an emotion comes up or when you are in a fight. You also feel the same when you make someone into a shadow figure and have them act out what you consider your darkest sins. Yet these are your projections and unconscious scripts. This issue within you may have escaped enough of your repression that it sometimes shows up in your world as another person. But what you see reflects **your** shadows that are imprisoned within, eating away at you. When a shadow shows up in your world, all the self-hatred you have for yourself is virulently turned toward this person. You keep forgetting that everything that shows up in your world is what you think of yourself. Your world is a giant mirror of your self-concepts. One of my early books called *50 Ways to Change Your Mind and Change the World* and the upcoming book *The World is Your Mirror* both cover this concept in depth. Every fight with another reflects a conflict of self-concepts within you. If you bring the inner fight to integration and wholeness, the outer fight dissolves.

Every fight makes your ego the hero. The fight is proof you need the ego, along with its attack and the defenses needed for your fights. Fights separate you from others, even as the ego increases the conflict within. What you attack in others, you split off even more in yourself. Your ego or self-identity is the principle of separation, so a fight goes exactly according to its plan. It has you judge and attack others, which leads to the experience of fear. It then sells you guns and many other defenses with which to protect yourself, and this leads to even more fear. Those who are heavily defended are attempting to dissociate the terror in their hearts by their defenses. Your guns and litigious society that are meant to protect you make you more frightened in the end. It's all a vicious circle.

When you attack it is obvious that you are in a fight, and attack comes from feelings of weakness. But there are other known forms of fighting that hide weakness, such as passive-aggression, in which you shoot at others from behind the rocks but have so much denial you don't even realize you are doing it. When you are passive-aggressive you don't understand why people are always backing away from you or 'unloading on you'.

Another form of attack on others is self-attack. The foundation of the ego is attack and self-attack. Concepts of guilt and sin always lead to self-punishment but as *A Course in Miracles* states: "Attack is not discrete." So every time you attack yourself, you attack others also. You deny that attack on yourself has an effect on others, and by being blind to it you don't change it. You hide a great deal from yourself because if you were aware of it, you would have to change it. Withdrawal is a form of attack that contains just as much fight energy as direct attack. Unfortunately, as soon as you withdraw, you go into sacrifice and have stepped back from life, success and relationships. Your stepping back is thus a stepping back from yourself, as well as another, in the fight.

Another major form of fighting you are unaware of occurs when you are victimized. Included in the self-attack of a victim situation, there is hidden attack, fighting and revenge. You hurt yourself or have others or life hurt you to get back at others. Any failure is actually a form of revenge. When you are victimized, you are fighting another, your essence, your Self.

Scarcity is a form of fighting that is hidden beneath what seems to be missing. Scarcity in anything, from love, money, success or health can fall under the category of what is missing in your life and therefore an aspect of how you fight. You blame someone for your condition while condemning others for it.

Firstly, *awareness* can help you in the face of so much attack, defense and denial. If you want to find out what is really going on with you, even if it is hidden deep within, you can do so by strong intention. Otherwise, you hide what is going on from yourself and attack the truth to protect your ego. Secondly, *the strong intention to discover what is hidden in the subconscious and unconscious* empowers you for blessed change. A sense of humor and taking yourself lightly helps when getting to know yourself at these deeper levels.

Thirdly, if you *take responsibility for your situations and emotions* and stop blaming your problems and emotions on others, it is a big step forward that helps you, others and the whole world. Fourth, if you *take an attitude of healing* so that you see no bad guys, just others needing help, it frees both you and others. Fifth, if you *forgive yourself for every fight and bad feeling*, you don't stay stuck in them. If you wouldn't accuse and condemn yourself, then everyone is shown understanding and mercy. Sixth, if you remember most of the people you fight or have fought with are *people you promised to help* and even save them from themselves as part of your purpose, then you have a different attitude when trouble springs up. When you no longer use people as an excuse to be wounded or righteous, or to separate, or to shrink from facing your fears of going forward, this helps your maturity and willingness. Your desire for the truth will free you of both pain and illusion.

The more emotionally mature you are, the more attractive and successful you are. Your personal happiness, relationship and career depend on this maturity. Your willingness brings flow, and flow is both good timing and luck.

Chapter 70

In a Fight, Look for Where You are Making the Mistake

In a fight, look for where you are making the mistake. Basically, in a fight, both people are making a mistake. Yet, if you point out the other's mistakes, it is because you are avoiding the mistakes you are making. And typically, when you point out the other's mistakes without dealing with your own, you just get into a bigger fight. So, if you are really interested in ending the fight, look for where you are making the mistake. Maturity always invites you to acknowledge your mistakes because as soon as you do, then your higher mind sets out to transform them. But first, it takes your acknowledgment. If the other does apologize and you don't, you will sooner or later look for somebody else to fight with. This is always a delay borne out of fear. Most fights are silly miscommunications that you can resolve by sharing. But when there is an old pattern, then healing must occur for there to be change. This could be as simple as you acknowledging your mistake and apologizing.

It takes two to fight. Once you acknowledge your mistake and step forward, the fight is over because you have moved on, unafraid to go forward. If you cannot see where you have made a mistake, then try forgiving yourself, the other and the situation. Forgive anyone from the past who comes to your mind in regard to this situation. The more you forgive, the clearer the situation will become.

Remember: "Issues are always equal in a relationship." You may be compensating and in denial and you may not be grossly acting out the issue as your partner is, but then you probably have better make-up. For instance, if your partner was unfaithful sexually, you were unfaithful to the same extent.

Possibly, you were dependent and mistook neediness for love and commitment. Somehow, your lack of trust equaled their lack of being trustworthy. Naiveté is not trust. Your denial then led to heartbreak. Your denial now leads to independence, sacrifice and victim roles. Buried under denial, it could take a bit of forgiveness to discover your collusion in any event.

Another example is when a partner seems to be using you. Either you were failing to help them as you promised at a soul level, or you may have been using them to hold yourself back. I have worked with people who were fighting someone from the past long after they had broken up with them and they still hadn't gone on with their life. They were still using the person to hold themselves back rather than simply learning the lesson and moving forward.

Now, it is time to be very clear and truthful in this fight if you want to free yourself and have peace.

Chapter 71

Emotions are Reactive and Instantaneous

Emotions are reactive, triggered by outside or inside stimuli. It is easier to notice a stimulus when it is outside rather than when it comes from inside you. When it comes from within, emotions like sadness, feeling bad or even angry, just seem to come up and you are not quite sure why. It is not necessary for you to know what tripped the wire that caused your emotions but when they come up, it is important to have the right attitude, which is: "This is something I am called to heal. I commit to healing it." If you commit to healing as a way of life, then you are much more likely to catch yourself and use every negative feeling and problem that comes up as an opportunity to heal. If you do this, you are much less likely to go into emotional indulgence, pollution or attack, whatever comes up.

Because emotions seem to be instantaneous, you think something outside you made you feel them. But if you could see the subconscious, you would know that you actually chose the situation, and what triggered it, to get the emotion out. The emotion has been stuck inside, and most of the time it just flashes out of you. Yet, before the flash, you made choices about the trigger you would employ, and then about whether you were going to use the emotion for healing or as a weapon. Your emotions show you what you have carried from the past and what is yet unhealed or unlearned in the present. When an emotion comes up, it is your chance to learn the lesson before it becomes a trial and to turn what was painful into wholeness.

Keep choosing for healing before, during and after emotional events and this will soon become a healing attitude. Don't be blindsided by your own emotions.

Commit to emotional intelligence. Your maturity is crucial to partnership, purpose and your destiny. If you don't grow up to be emotionally mature, you will let off toxic emotional elements and pollute those around you with attack, when instead you could be inspiring others with your attitude and your healing. You can either go for happiness or emotional indulgence but you can't have both and you get to decide which path you will follow.

Chapter 72

In a Fight, Give Up Winning and Being Right

A fight is a competition that has turned into a power struggle. Equality is missing and you think you would gain something by dominating the other and having your way but the desire to win over another is shortsighted. You don't realize that if you beat your partner now, they will look for ways to beat or ambush you so they could win for a change. Or, worse yet, they would give up and adjust to the situation, leaving a chronically dead relationship that the ego has convinced you is good because you are in control. Winning over your partner delays you and stultifies the relationship. Any attempt at winning shows you have confused winning with success. Success means a step forward while winning doesn't necessarily mean a step forward at all, simply a step in dominating another.

In a fight, you act as if you are right and your attacks come from righteous anger. If you gave up being right, you would be open to learn instead. A fight means you have closed down in some way. You could use the fight as a first step to know there is something to learn and a step to take forward. As you give up the fight, you could see what the lesson was that was waiting for you. If you weren't being right, and therefore closed, there would be no fight because there would be nothing to defend. Truth doesn't need defense and the so-called 'right' you attempted to defend was just what your ego was invested in and got you to do the dirty work of its fighting for it. Now, it's time to let go of being right so you can move forward together beyond the fight, valuing partnership more than righteousness, which was really a cover for something you felt guilty about.

Chapter 73

In a Fight, You are Acting in Opposite Ways

In a fight, each party is typically acting in an opposite way, but feeling the same thing. If you recognize that in spite of the other's behavior they are actually feeling the same thing as you, then you have the first step in the understanding, compassion and rapport needed to end your fight amicably.

The next time you are in a fight with someone, check in with what you are feeling and use that as a barometer as to what they may be experiencing also. Begin to respond to that feeling in them because if you have the same feeling, you understand what it's like to feel that and can respond empathically.

I remember a blind date I had gone on in 1975. I went to pick up the woman at her place and we were chatting for a while as we were getting to know each other. Then, from out of the blue, the woman began verbally attacking me. After a few minutes, I went within and noticed I was feeling fear. So I asked her, "Are you feeling fear?"

And she replied, "Yeah, I'm feeling fear."

I said, "Yeah, me too!"

As a result, the attack ended and we could communicate easily with each other again. We talked for another 30 minutes and then I got up to leave.

The woman said, "I guess this means you aren't going to call me again."

I said, "Yes. That would be right." Yet there was a sense of success about the night because we had bridged what otherwise would have been a fight. Though there wasn't anything there to take the meeting further, I had saved both of us a very awkward and potentially painful situation.

Many times, people's behavior and your interpretation of what they are feeling leads you to judge them. But if you felt what you were feeling and understood that's what they were feeling, it could lead you to extend yourself to them and end the attack as you begin communicating.

Chapter 74

The Power of Choice

You don't realize that moment by moment you are making a choice between Heaven and hell. You can tell which one you choose by how you feel. If you are choosing love no matter what the rest of the world is doing around you, what is negative around you won't touch you. Choose love enough times and you begin to radiate out love in such a way that you start to transform the world around you. If you choose to love and to give when you are in pain, then you begin to heal the pain layer by layer till it's gone.

You can look out at the world and realize that no matter what is going on you can choose peace. "I could have peace instead of this" is a line from *A Course in Miracles* that if chosen again and again, begins to change your perception and experience of the world.

If you choose for the ego, you will suffer and this suffering is how you know you made a mistake. Of course, every time you suffer, you consciously or subconsciously believe that it's another's fault that you are suffering. This bit of ego defense won't keep you out of pain, though you will judge and have grievances toward others because you projected on them what you were doing, as well as your beliefs about yourself. Your judgment and grievances take you deeper and deeper into pain and problems. Instead of this, you could choose to remember God. By doing this, you remember yourself as spirit, which in turn reminds you that everything is yours for the asking.

Today and every day, keep your attention on love, peace and being a Child of God. Choose it moment by moment and your happiness will build. On the other hand, be aware whenever you have gone off track and again and again choose to have peace instead.

Your power of choice is simply whether you will choose to listen to your ego or your higher mind. Every good thing comes to you through choosing to listen to your higher mind, while the negativity you experience means you listened and invested in the ego's guidance. Either way, you get to choose. What is it that you want?

Chapter 75

The Power Beyond Choice

While the power to choose is your greatest power here, it is limited to choosing whether you will listen to the ego or your higher mind. This prerogative to choose is held onto dearly by the ego. It attributes choice to itself. On the other hand, as you let go of more and more personalities and self-concepts, you become ever more content to follow the Tao, the unfolding process that is leading to ever greater wholeness. This is the Holy Spirit who uses time to break you free of time. Time is for healing and finding your way back to wholeness.

There is a much greater power than your own power to choose. It is the power that comes of the Tao unfolding in time and leading you back to Heaven. The power beyond choice is to choose to give up your power of choice and let the Holy Spirit decide for you as you float on the Tao, carried along in the most positive fashion. Do you want your way, or for the best way to become your way, as you let Heaven make the best choice? Heaven would never ask you to sacrifice, while on the other hand sacrifice is one of the chief attributes of your ego.

Chapter 76

The Path of Atonement

The "path of atonement" is a phrase from A *Course in Miracles* to describe the path of healing that leads to wholeness and peace. It states that time is meant to be used for healing as this restores us to greater peace and wholeness. It is a path of ever greater happiness, innocence and centeredness. Choosing this path will lead you to Heaven on earth.

Your emotions show you where you are meant to heal. It shows you where you have made a mistake. It shows you where you chose to frame another and blanket your attack under a victim's disguise. It shows where you chose to hide rather than step up, where you separated rather than joined and where you judged rather than helped. You took on the mantle of sacrifice and need in order to dissemble the independence you sought and wrongly thought would make you happy. An emotion shows where you blamed and framed another to show that it was them and not you who were guilty. An emotion shows all of this and more. Most of all, it shows where you are in need of correction. You could ask Heaven's grace to correct your mind to innocence, which you will know because everyone will likewise be innocent. You could forgive yourself your trespasses as you forgive those you set up to trespass against you. You could commit to the path of atonement as your path to freeing yourself. It is this path that will lead you to even greater wholeness and happiness. As your peace grows, it is shared with those around you, bringing all that is great in life. By committing to the path of atonement, you have an attitude that will more and more heal the illusions of your life and eventually bring you to Oneness.

Chapter 77

In a Fight, You are Called Upon to Give

In a fight, the other person experiences lack and if you fight back, you believe you are in lack also. On the other hand, you could give to them to heal the lack in them. In so doing, you recognize your abundance and bring peace where there was strife. It is simple to give to someone. You could keep blessing them. You could send love or peace to them. You could ask yourself what it is that they need. Any situation you are in, you have the exact gift needed to resolve the situation. Ask what that is and open the door in your mind to that gift. Fill yourself with it and then pour it into that person. You could also ask how old is the wounded self that feels it needs to fight. Pour love into that person or child and it will grow up to the person's present age and integrate into them, generating peace and wholeness.

You could ask for Heaven's help and receive whatever Heaven wanted to give you for this person. After you have received it, then pour that gift into them. Usually, a person who is fighting is wide open at a gut-level. Their aggressive energy hides that but it is shown to those who want to help. It is easy to pour in whatever you wish at this level.

If you realize that the person fighting with you is in need of help, it makes it much easier for you to respond to that call for help. If you refuse it, you are making the same mistake they are and feel weak and in lack and you stay stuck or regress. If, on the other hand, you help them, then you are both freed and there is a step forward and a flow for both.

Gifts that are shared create flow both for you and for the other with whom the gifts are shared.

It is not Heaven's Will nor is it your true will to fight. It destroys your peace, the foundation of love and happiness and instead, through attack and self-attack, builds the foundation of the ego. Choose for your true will and God's Will because only those together will make you happy.

Chapter 78

The Proper Use of Sensitivity

So many of you are sensitive and some of you are overly sensitive. The more sensitive you are the easier it is for you to get hurt or heartbroken, but there is a way to prevent that. If you don't, you will find yourself withdrawing and getting your toes stepped on as you become more allergic to the world around you. Being oversensitive makes it hard to please you and you can find yourself easily irritated. It is easy to become fractious, demanding and complaining. This is obviously the wrong use of your sensitivity, which is really an antenna.

The way to keep from getting hurt is to focus your sensitivity so that it is used for gifts in relationships and your work. It can all be put toward your function, and the best way to keep from misusing it is to turn it over to Heaven so you don't use it for specialness or trying to get attention. Once your sensitivity is focused, which occurs through your choice, then the next step is to turn it over to Heaven and see what gift emerges. Gifts help you and those around you. They set you into a flow, make things easier and fulfill you. The more you do this and do not use your sensitivity in a mistaken way to take, then gifts keep developing and your sensitivity leads to elegance, beauty and extending yourself, rather than to the dark glamour of being wounded and calling attention to yourself.

True sensitivity helps you feel into others and situations. Used correctly, your sensitivity develops into artistic, psychic and healing gifts. It adds to your awareness and it leads to fineness in your life and the lives of those around you.

Chapter 79

If You are in a Fight, You are Called to Change Your Perception

If you are in a fight, you are called upon to change your perception of what is taking place. You are responsible for what you see because it comes from your choices, your beliefs and your thoughts, all of which you are responsible for and all of which have an effect on your perception and thus your experience of the world.

This is what the subconscious shows: what you see is what you choose to see. It comes from your invitation. The choice is made by your ego but through healing you could melt away the walls of the ego, bringing more flow. It is the dissolution of the ego, and the world it perceives, that is the real goal that brings a joy beyond joy. It is the path of healing that transforms negative perception, and finally all perception, to Heaven on earth. Naturally, you deny and hide a great deal in your subconscious and unconscious, especially aggression. Your choice for a fight sides with your ego rather than your higher mind. This is a choice for separation, independence and attack. It is an attempt to gain control, blame another, be right, attack yourself and others, and generally build the ego. On the other side, there could have been a choice for your higher mind, where there are gifts, grace, your purpose and destiny. But your fear of shining and your desire to stay small led you to invest in your ego. All the separation has built up so you attempt to shift the pressure by displacing it on others. Now is the time to change your perception, firstly by taking responsibility for what you see and experience. Secondly, you can consciously choose to have peace and love instead of what you are experiencing. If you look at the scene and notice what you feel, you could declare, "I want peace and love instead of what I see and feel."

Then notice if the feeling got better or worse. Also see how it looks. If it gets worse, it is just impacted feelings coming up from deep within. Again, choose: "I want peace and love instead of what I see and feel."

Once again, notice how it looks and feels and once more declare: "I want peace and love instead of what I see and feel."

Again, notice how it seems to you and once more choose: "I want peace and love instead of what I see and feel."

At some point, it starts to look and feel better. Keep choosing to have love and peace until the situation looks and feels like the 'Garden'. Use this on present problems or bad feelings and use it on past painful situations in your life to transform them and their self-defeating patterns.

Chapter 80

In a Fight, There is a Choice to Displace Your Anger

In a fight, you displace your anger on the one you are fighting with. You can't stand the pressure, stress or feelings that build up in you with anger, so you look to get rid of these emotions by dumping them on another. Also, guilt leads to attack and self-attack. The self-attack shows up as you use the other as an instrument to attack yourself. Every time you separated, the attack you made from guilt, and therefore anger, built up inside you. And though much of it is suppressed or repressed within you, you have been accumulating anger since the Fall. At times you blame others for pushing you away, but this is only to hide your desire to separate.

You can't have love and anger at the same time; only one or the other. You can't remember God or have a Golden Life when you have attack. You must relinquish the anger as a mistake because this is what the ego has used to build itself.

A fight is the perfect opportunity to dump anger on another that has nothing to do with them except that subconsciously they feel they deserve it. Also, what you are angry at them about is what you are doing. Now, it is time to become aware of all of the forms anger can take and let it go as a mistake. The extent you feel innocent is the extent you let go of the attack on yourself and others. It is time to let go of your anger so you can have love, the Garden and God back in your life.

Chapter 81

In a Fight, You are Called to Choose Again

Every fight is an answer to the ego's call to separate and not go forward. The fight means you've fallen for the bait of the ego and you are replaying an old mistake. Yet, if you turn away from the fight and choose again, you will find ample support from your higher mind. If you are committed to a healing path, then what comes up is simply the next thing to heal. Being on a healing path, you have already made the choice to turn to the light and each time you adhere to it, the decision becomes automatic and you nip the fight in the bud.

You can choose again for truth and healing as you are willing to open the door in your mind for your soul gift, accepting Heaven's grace and miracles. You can embrace your purpose and destiny, each of which has the ability to turn both sides in a fight into a new wholeness where there is peace and mutual success.

A fight shows a pattern based on an old decision. You can reverse the decision that had you separate so that you begin to realize the only way forward is together rather than fighting. By joining, the other brings the energy and the piece needed to make greater wholeness for both of you. This only happens if you choose to join the other. You don't have to agree with them to join them but in joining them an integration occurs that presents the best way. Choose again. Value peace more than your ego and its values, which lead you nowhere. Specialness, attention, dark glamour, projection, being right, attack, self-attack, winning, and fear of the next step are all distracting, delaying and self-defeating. You could have peace instead. Keep choosing peace to get through all the layers of fighting.

Chapter 82

In a Fight, There is a Way for Both to Win

In a fight, there is a way for both parties to win, not only now, but forever. How this is accomplished is to realize that it is possible, and to call on Heaven or the Holy Spirit. The inspiration that comes to you from beyond time can be very practical. It can take you step by step or right to the heart of what is needed. A sincere invitation brings in the guidance that is needed for there to be equality and mutuality. Ask for this inspiration. Want it with all your heart. Let it show you the way for both of you to leap forward. You are all evolving toward radical trust, to become like little children once more. This is mastery, and beyond, on the evolutionary scale. As Jesus said, "Unless you become like little children, you cannot enter the Kingdom of Heaven." Turn over the tiller of your life to Heaven so you can become carefree and open to all the help and answers Heaven has for you to leap forward together.

Today, relax deeply by resting in God. When your mind is quiet ask for guidance or direction. Whatever message you receive, let grace do it for you. Finding the way in which both can win, which is Heaven's way, can save you so much time. If one person feels like they have lost, then the fight will come up again and again. Let wholeness, mutuality and equality bless you both. Heaven is on your side to find a way in which you both can win. You are both equally loved by Heaven. Heaven will bless you with a way if you will only listen. In the solution is the confidence to succeed at a whole new level for both of you. Why waste time when the answer is here now? When your desire for it is stronger than your fear to have it, you will have it. So relax in quiet because peace heals fear and the answer can be there for both of you. Relax into Heaven's arms and let the peace renew and open you.

Chapter 83

An Attack is a Call for Help

An attack is a call for help, as all that is not love is a call for love. To attack is to side with the ego's feeling that you are weak and not good enough. Attack is the desire to make yourself equal or better but attack cannot accomplish this and this can never work. The ego makes you weak through self-attack and then offers its help to make you stronger, suggesting you attack. This builds the ego and generates guilt, fear, power struggle and revenge, all of which build the ego. On the other hand, the path of healing leads to wholeness and peace. And it is from peace that love, abundance and all good things flow.

You are constantly choosing between building the ego and reclaiming your wholeness. As you help, you realize that there is help you can avail yourself of if ever you need help yourself. If you feel your ego needs defense when someone attacks, then you withdraw or attack back. But if you realize that the ego and its self-concepts are not worth defending, you could choose the path of healing instead. When you choose for the ego, you split your mind and make yourself less worthy. The ego uses this to disown you as being beneath it. It condemns you to death and only waits to carry out your sentence. If you choose the healing path, you know that everyone is important, either for the support they give you or for what they mirror back to you of what needs to be healed within.

Chapter 84

Whenever You are Unhappy, You are Trying to Be Right

All of your belief systems limit you. Of course, the negative beliefs are much more destructive and limiting than the positive, so it is important to get rid of them first. You have made your belief systems through thoughts that you invested your faith in. It is these belief systems that are also constellations of personalities, because every belief or concept is a self-concept. Every self-concept is like being wrapped in a giant condom. They limit contact and stop the flow. They give us recipes about how to look at the world.

Beliefs determine your perception and experience. It's not so much 'seeing is believing' as believing is seeing. What you see simply reinforces your beliefs because what you experience occurs according to how you believe it will be. Anything you made, you were invested in. You want to be right about what you invested yourself in because it is your own character you have made, along with the world you perceive.

All of these beliefs and self-concepts are separations, and separation induces pain, fear and guilt. Being right is the defense you use to try to keep the pain, fear and guilt at bay. All of these self-concepts stop the flow, and belief systems narrow the reality of what is possible. A belief system can cause a log jam in the flow of your life as well as a lot of dissociation that comes from the disconnection of your self-concepts. If you are unhappy, the flow is stopped. "You cannot be right and be happy too" is a statement from *A Course in Miracles*. Where you are unhappy, you are trying to be right, to hold onto your beliefs and avoid openness to a deeper reality that is not negative. Whenever you are less than happy, turn your mind over to Heaven by opening yourself to a greater spiritual reality that is based on love and happiness. Allow yourself to be moved beyond your beliefs and limitations and experience the world in a whole new way. Life can be as big as you allow it to be. Give up where you are trying to be right about yourself, others and life.

Ask yourself what beliefs about yourself are making you unhappy.

Ask yourself what beliefs you have about others that are making you unhappy.

Ask yourself what belief you have about life that is making you unhappy.

Whatever beliefs 'pop' into your mind about yourself, others and life, be willing to let them go so you are open once again for happiness.

Chapter 85

In a Fight, You are Called to Heal Fear

Fights generate fear because they are full of attack and self-attack. You think the attack you make on yourself hurts you. As a result, you then think the attack you make on another, and that they make on you, has effects that hurt you. This generates lots of fear but if you want to side with Heaven and not with the ego, you will concentrate on healing the fear and the attack. The key is not to be afraid of the fear because it is in facing the fear that it is resolved, just as when you turn toward the sun the shadows disappear while if you turn away from the sun, the shadows lengthen before you.

If you face the fear, you will find beliefs and belief systems that the fear is defending. It is these self-concepts that the ego is defending because this is what the ego is made out of, and it is fighting for its life. Beliefs show investment in the ego. You are attached to them because you made them. You have hidden them from yourself, but now is the time to see if you really want them. All of these concepts, which are ultimately self-concepts, were built at the expense of your self-worth because they came about through splitting your mind as you broke bonding. Your lack of self-worth is what the ego uses to condemn you to death. The ego thinks that one of you has to die. It is either it or you. It doesn't really trust you because it thinks, and rightly so, that you will betray it for Heaven. The ego therefore gets you to believe you are a body and, as a result, on your way to death, rather than have you realize that you are eternal spirit. The ego wants to kill you and though it has delivered the death sentence, it may wait a while to carry it out and entertain itself with a little torture on the way. This is why it is crucial to examine your beliefs and belief-systems that are generating fear to protect the ego. Is it really worth it to have this identity? Is this what you want when you could recognize yourself as eternal, unlimited spirit? Then you would not need negative beliefs, or even positive beliefs to compensate for your negative beliefs, especially when they are the source of fear and valuelessness.

So, when you have fear, face it and go beneath to see what it defends. Then choose to see if these beliefs are worth it and if they are what you really want, because these beliefs carry a death sentence with them.

As you heal the fear, you recognize attack for what it is – the ego making a play to own your life and eventually ending it.

Chapter 86

Loss Gives Rise to Fear

Loss comes from separation and gives rise to fear. You don't realize that when you are in a relationship and someone leaves you or leaves their body, you do not have to disconnect with them. The sorrow and hurt you feel is the part of you that was both separated and attached or fused but not bonded. So, when you do suffer a loss, you could realize that you do not have to suffer. You could join and bond with the person in their leaving. This brings the feeling of love, and does not hold you back like the suffering that signals attachment. Letting go generates a feeling of tenderness as sorrow is let go of. As Shakespeare said through Romeo: "...parting is such sweet sorrow."

When loss occurs and is not let go of, you look to the future and see what is coming as similar to the past. You look at the future through eyes of the past so if you have sadness, a sure sign you haven't completed your letting go, then you will also be frightened to the same extent. When you have completed your emotional healing of the past, then all that remains is peace, flow and blessings. Otherwise, you will feel anxious and fearful. Both loss and fear are fruits of your separating but other emotions are there also and include feeling abandoned, inadequate, hurt and guilty. Actually, all of your emotions speak of you separating or an old separation coming to the surface.

One of my favorite ways of healing loss and fear is to put my future in the Hands of God, which are words from *A Course in Miracles*. As you choose this layer by layer, the peace and flow can come to you at deeper and deeper levels. From this loss, a rebirth will occur with all the love, gratitude and poignancy that occurs from letting go.

Chapter 87

In a Fight, Head Toward Your Partner

If you are in a fight, you have invested in your ego's purpose of separation. This is the opposite direction you want to go in if you want new levels of success and intimacy. Your ego gets fat during fights. You are investing in self-concepts and a certain personality but what is called for is to invest in life, specifically *your* life. If you win and they lose, your partner or opponent loses value and you lose equality, which makes them less attractive. So you lose as they become dependent on you. This puts you both in sacrifice. On the other hand, the direction of success and intimacy is toward your partner or your opponent. Be brave about any emotions you have to go through to reach them. While it may look like these emotions are their feelings, they are also yours. It behoves you to heal these and you do so simply by heading toward and joining your partner or opponent in this. Your ego's purpose with these emotions was to keep separation in place. This keeps the ego strong and problems intact.

All of this can change by your commitment to your partner, no matter what is occurring, and not just your partner but anyone you are having a conflict with. Anyone can be joined with and this moves you on to the next step forward in success. Joining another by always reaching out to them becomes the path of repairing your value and that of others. This heals both of you, as extending yourself gives you self-value and this self-value becomes self-love. So when you give to another by heading toward them to join in partnership, your giving is an act of both valuing and loving them. This melts aspects of your ego and theirs, letting more life and abundance in. This type of extending yourself adds to both the health and flow in your life.

Heading toward your partner re-establishes your goal for happiness for yourself. You are choosing not to build your ego, which would make it strong and you weak, eventually ending in misery for you with lots of attack and self-attack along the way. When you reach your partner, you pop to the next layer of success and intimacy. At times, this can mean falling into the next layer of what needs to be healed but, since the fight is over, this is much easier, even if the next layer that comes up for healing is a soul wound. In a fight, let your goal be the other because this builds mutuality, one of the key elements of success.

Chapter 88

Fighting Begins with Self-Attack

When you attack yourself, you believe that it has some effect. You believe it weakens you. This is both the essence and fallacy of all attack. Because you believe it weakened you, you then believe that it will weaken another. And having weakened yourself, you believe you are less than another. You then attack them to put them at the same level or below you. If the other seems weakened by your attack, it reinforces the idea that attack weakens. Your self-attack and belief that it weakens you betrays the invulnerability that comes of recognizing yourself as spirit. Self-attack strikes at the experience of your wholeness, splits your mind and you begin to believe that you are weak, as a split mind is an investment in weakness. Having used attack on yourself, you then turn it on others.

Every attack begins with self-attack and this is where the ego as the principle of separation begins to construct itself. If you could recognize yourself as whole or as invulnerable spirit, you would see the attack on yourself as ineffective. The whole basis of attack would be undermined because if it didn't work on you, then you won't use it on another. If you value peace, wholeness and yourself as spirit, you could never see yourself as weak or needing to equalize any situation. Attack and self-attack are seen as useless.

Give up all self-attack and, even more, do not invest in the belief that it weakens you. You only invest in this self-attack and attack because you want to make a world of your own with your belief and this separates you from Oneness or Heaven. As you begin to realize that all you want is God and His Love, you begin to invest in harmlessness, self-forgiveness and dismantling the world you made for the one God created that contains no attack and therefore no suffering.

This is an important lesson in giving up fights. You can't fight with another unless you have already begun fighting with yourself and thinking that it wounded you.

Chapter 89

In a Fight, You are Called Upon to Forgive

In a fight, you are called upon to forgive because what you see is only what you think of yourself. How you respond to another is how you respond to yourself. To forgive another is to forgive yourself, releasing hidden guilt that has held you back. The conflict this fight represents is fed by guilt and fear and released by forgiveness.

If you can look at another and choose not to condemn yourself for what you perceive in them, you are both freed. If you could realize the other is in need and they represent your hidden need for help, it would help you both. To respond to them, bringing them back their innocence and thus bringing your innocence back at even deeper levels frees you, them and the world.

In truth, you need the other to see what needs healing in you, not through cobbling yourself together but by the joining that forgiveness brings. This joining shows mutual interests are in your own best interest. And your gratitude is due to the other for showing you what you so successfully hid that can now be healed.

So bring your forgiveness and gratitude to whomever seems to oppose you because these are the hidden caches of darkness in your mind that need the release of light.

Chapter 90

In a Fight, You are Called to Wholeness

A fight means you are caught in polarity. One of your sides fights against the other. Yet, each side contains half of the answer. This is notwithstanding that one of the parties in this fight might be totally mistaken in what they are doing, but they are still needed to make a whole. That you are fighting with another says that you judged and split off that part of yourself that they represent for you. You need that part back without the judgment. There needs to be a joining or integration that is really a re-integration to achieve peace and greater wholeness. When all of these splits have been re-integrated, you will experience Oneness once more. The wholeness achieved as you evolve brings more power and innocence with each step, as well as less conflict.

Your commitment to wholeness in any conflict wins valuable pieces of yourself back that you have fractured and made wrong. If you hadn't, there would be no fight. Once you join the other and you don't necessarily have to agree with their position to do this, then you reach beyond the fight and there is a flow forward once more. This level of the separation is over and, as a result, some of the guilt and fear in each of you is healed. There is a bit more togetherness until the next split emerges as a conflict. Each fight represents an opportunity for greater wholeness, which lends itself to greater success, as well as greater intimacy. Each relationship gives you the opportunity to go beyond where you have limited yourself with this egoistic desire to separate.

Now, it's time to reverse all your fights, win yourself back and bring the awareness and flow that comes of greater wholeness.

Chapter 91

In a Fight, Look for Your Hidden Plan

In a fight, look for your hidden plan. It has already been noted how a fight is about getting needs met and trying to be right when at least part of you feels wrong. You also use a fight to try to protect yourself from fear by not taking the next step. Actually, it is only by taking the next step that you heal fear. To move through fear, face what frightens you and move beyond it. Yet, there are other aspects to discover and heal about fights and if you use your intuition, you can make the subconscious conscious and thus move past your denial and get your power back.

See if you can get an answer for each of the following questions before you move onto the next. The best answers leap straight to mind because of your willingness. All of these questions have answers to them. Some answers will be more important than others but they can all help you piece together what you had hidden from yourself. Then, with your conscious mind, you can choose if you want to side with your higher mind and use the situation for peace or side with your ego and exacerbate this pattern.

Ask yourself these questions:

What am I using this fight for?

What am I trying to get from this fight?

There are probably layers to this next question.

What am I afraid to lose that I felt I had to fight to keep?

What am I hiding from by having this fight?

What am I afraid of?

This fight is a cover for a deeper fight. Who else am I fighting with?

What is the purpose of this fight?

What are the payoffs of this fight?

Besides the person I am fighting with, who else am I making wrong?

What is this about?

What am I being right about?

What does this fight allow me to do?

What does this fight allow me not to do?

What am I proving by this fight?

What am I trying to control about myself by having this fight?

Who else am I trying to control by this fight?

Why am I trying to control them?

What excuse does this fight give me?

What aspect of my purpose do I get to avoid by this fight?

What did I think the separation resulting from this fight would give me?

What is the guilt and failure on my part that led to this fight?

Who am I trying to get attention from by having this fight?

Many times, when you discover the hidden elements, you can let go of both these elements and the fight itself. If not, keep forgiving yourself and others until you reach the profound peace that signals the fight is over.

Chapter 92

When You Feel Innocent, You Perceive Everyone's Innocence

When you feel innocent, you extend yourself in love. You perceive everyone's innocence because you see what you think you are. Perception is filtered through your self-concepts. The more self-concepts you have, the more guilt you have because each self-concept separates you and separation generates fear, pain and guilt. Innocence, on the other hand, is wholeness and comes from Wholeness Itself. When you feel innocent, you still see problems and mistakes but most of all you experience compassion for mistakes and the people who make them. Guilt, however, sees wrong-doing and desires to punish it. Both judgment and punishment are attempts to keep the wrong you see outside, but feel inside, as far away as possible.

Everyone feels guilty, but innocence is the truth. Without innocence, you will not learn the lesson nor correct the mistakes. Guilt leads to attack and self-attack, moving you further from wholeness and guidance. Having gone in the wrong direction, you move away from yourself, your Self and Heaven. You set up patterns that prove both painful and self-defeating, investing in the ego's will of separation and attack, rather than your true will. The more innocent you become, the more abundant you allow yourself to be. Your innocence teaches innocence and blesses the world by its example. Innocence promulgates understanding, which is the very foundation of healing and the means to wholeness.

Even if you feel guilt, with its ancillary emotion of unworthiness, it is neither psychologically nor spiritually true. It is not true psychologically as it can be healed and returned to wholeness, as all emotions can. Spiritually, you were created as spirit by God and this cannot be changed. You can only pile self-concepts on yourself, building an ego as if you had really changed something. You only believed this change could happen. This led you deeper into the dream of time, built on separation and guilt, and only unraveling into eternity once more when you become totally innocent having accepted the truth about yourself.

Commit to your innocence and you commit to everyone's innocence. Commit to innocence and you commit to love and a world that is safe, healed and whole. All evolution is marked by ever greater innocence and the same is true of higher consciousness. Innocence and truth are synonymous. God is Truth, Innocence and Oneness. This is the direction everyone is heading toward sooner or later. Why not let it be sooner?

Chapter 93

In a Fight, Emotions are Part of the Fight

In a fight, the emotions you feel are what you think comes about because of what the other is doing. Yet, they are actually coming from what you are doing. They are part of your arsenal of weapons that you use to defend yourself. They themselves are a form of attack. If you had a totally different attitude you would use the emotion or dissociation for you to realize what needs healing. When you have dissociation, you give up the form of control your emotion is attempting to get because you think the dissociation will give you even more control. Yet both your emotions and dissociation are different weapons you use to gain control or the upper hand. Partnership, on the other hand, comes from joining and sharing: they give you confidence rather than control.

Weapons beg to be used to prove their usefulness and to give them a reason for being. Emotions are weapons that are forms of attack. Peace, however, guarantees a safety that emotions never could. Peace invites love, sharing and relatedness. Emotions state that you are not only at odds with another, you are at odds with yourself. This fight and its emotions show not only attack, but self-attack. They reflect a place where you do not love yourself. To love yourself is to heal yourself. This dissolves the emotion and makes you available to others in a way that invites connection and friendship. When a car is not running right, you see that this is so by the kinds of problems it has. An emotion is similar in that it is a signal that something is not running right within you.

Chapter 94

In a Fight, Your Outer Conflict Comes From an Inner One

The world mirrors your mind. When you are having a fight with someone, you are having a fight with yourself. The inner conflict has spilled over into the outer plane. The person or situation you are fighting on the outside reflects the less identified part of your mind. This is the part typically relegated to your subconscious or even your unconscious mind. It is dissociated, hidden and denied. You fight against it. It seems to attack you. This is really an ego fight between two self-concepts. It may even be a war between constellations of personalities. At any rate, it is all you, so the more you forgive the other, the more you move into mutuality and harmony with them and yourself. Besides forgiveness, acceptance can be an even more basic healing principle. What you accept heals your resistance and your fight. What you fought against is then let go of and this falls into perspective in your life rather than being right in your face. It then puts you back in the flow once more rather than using the fight to hide your fear. Integration of what the other represents helps you move into a new wholeness. This can be done simply by imagining one hand holding their position and your other hand holding your position. Melt these positions and self-concepts down to their pure light energy and bring both together. Only in their present form did they seem to conflict. Next, put the combined light and energy into your heart.

There may be other aspects that come up to accept, forgive and integrate but all of these principles help you move past the fear and into a new and better place.

Chapter 95

In a Fight, You are Called to Heal

A fight is a signal that something is amiss and needs healing. There may be wrongdoing on the other's part but if you get righteous about the situation, you lose the opportunity for healing on both the everyday and deeper levels of the mind. To heal these deeper layers now is to prevent further conflict down the road. You know your healing is complete when you are in a state of peace. Peace leads to love, abundance and joy so whenever you are without peace, you are cheating yourself of these aspects of good fortune. You can turn any fight or misfortune into good fortune through healing. To lose your peace is to lose the quiet mind necessary to hear the guidance that will show you how everyone can win, now and in the future. To get over a fight, it is crucial to realize there are no 'bad guys', only ignorant ones. A fight is always an attempt to delay yourself out of fear and, as a result, you can miss the opportunity of leaping forward.

Each fight is an opportunity to heal and have success and partnership where you have conflict. Don't stop your forgiveness until you are at peace and, if other layers come up in the future, then forgive them until you are centered and in peace. This is what the world is for - healing. Your fight is just one more opportunity to heal a big piece of your mind and achieve greater confidence and an expanded heart. Healing brings meaning to a meaningless world and recovers meaning that has been lost from old wounds, which are symptoms of old fights still going on. Commit to healing. Commit to yourself and the next step. Use no one to hold yourself back. Want only the wholeness that comes of healing because from it comes all good things.

A fight is a mistake and if you let yourself indulge in it, it could easily become a bad or righteous attitude on your part. When a fight begins, learning stops and learning and healing are two different sides of the same coin. In a fight, you are blindly caught up in yourself and nothing changes for the better. It is time to get over yourself so new chapters can begin. In a fight, you get caught up in the other's guilt and hide your own. Choose healing instead. Life is not all about you or your grievances. Your grievances are just another way to make life all about you in a situation. If you could see your subconscious, you would know how split and dishonest your conscious mind is. Choose healing now and bring what is hidden to light for healing with acceptance, forgiveness and integration.

Chapter 96

In a Fight, You are Both Parties

Rumi said: "You are the mirror and the face in it." The world is your mirror. It shows you your thoughts. It reflects your mind. It is the movie of your self-concepts. You are every character. You people the world with your past. The world shows you what you believe about yourself. Your mother, father, partner and children as well as ex-partners and siblings show you key parts of your soul-belief systems that you want to integrate so the gifts are shared and the problems are dissolved.

You are the protagonist and the antagonist in a fight. The antagonist shows you the less identified part of your mind but the outer conflict reflects an inner conflict. Everything you do to another, you do to yourself. Anything you say to another, you are telling to yourself. Inner and outer conflicts generate fear and this stops you from moving forward. As you accept, forgive, integrate and commit to another, there is a corresponding healing within you, and you move toward greater unity. Unity consciousness is one of joy and the recognition at a mind level that you and everyone are all one tapestry. Today recognize the other as yourself. Help them as you would help yourself and love them as you would love yourself.

Chapter 97

In a Fight, You are Called to Be Defenseless

Being defenseless seems to be counter to your natural reaction and need to defend yourself. Certainly, if you are attacked physically, you are called to defend yourself because letting yourself be physically hurt is not the truth. It would simply make both of you feel guilty. Yet, when you are attacked any other way, you are called to be defenseless. First of all, the truth doesn't need defending. Clarification can be a big help. Many times disagreements come about as a matter of misunderstandings that are easily resolved through sharing what each of you felt was going on.

If you are interested in healing so that you can experience a greater wholeness, then you would naturally be interested in defenselessness. It brings emotional maturity and invites partnership. If you are tempted to defend, ask yourself just what is it you are defending. It is probably your ego. With your permission and investment, your ego helped set up the attack because that is what the ego does. Defenselessness is the opposite of attack. It takes responsibility for the attack, realizing it wasn't some outside factor, like how wrong the other person was, that caused the problem, but somehow, the event was your choice that occurred through going along with the ego. The ego is the dynamic and principle of separation and it builds itself in conflict. Separation, like attack, generates fear and while the ego seeks to ingratiate itself by lessening fear, fear is one of its chief components. To get rid of fear would be to get rid of itself so it does this only in a limited fashion. Only in a fearful, separated world does the ego gain the autonomy it desperately seeks to attempt to make itself real. When you are attacked, ask yourself, "Just what is it that needs defending?" What is it that you are trying to prove? Any emotions that come up are emotions already inside you from the past. They are walls between you and yourself, you and success, you and those you love, and you and Heaven. It is time to heal the past and come to greater wholeness. These emotions represent mistakes that can be corrected. You can do this by giving. When anyone attacks, they are feeling weak and feel that they need something. If you remain as centered as possible, you can pour love, or whatever it is they need, into them energetically. Usually, people are wide open at a gut level when they attack. Even if their attack persists, and many times it doesn't, it is usually the last time they will attack to this degree.

When attack occurs, unless you begin to defend your ego you can simply witness what is occurring. This allows you to heal later at a more peaceful time any emotion that still remains. You don't have to defend yourself. You can imagine that you are smoke and the attack passes through you. You can ask that you and the other be carried back to ever deeper and higher centers. This allows you to bring the situation to ever greater peace that generates more love and togetherness.

In a fight, the other reflects belief systems you have invested in but denied. Ask yourself what you would have to believe in for this situation to be taking place or to have the other take the position they are in. Let go of these belief systems. They began with a choice and you can regain greater freedom by letting them go.

Finally, the other in a fight represents your hidden self-concepts. If you are defenseless, these self-concepts are naturally accepted, let go of and integrated. This opens you to a new level of partnership with the other.

What a person shows to you is what you were showing to them, so a lot of your hidden judgment and attack reveals itself. These hidden aspects are mistaken and can be easily let go of if you realize that they are generating attack toward yourself, as well as the fear, which shrinks your life. It is time to commit to defenselessness.

Chapter 98

Healing Through Love

Whenever you suffer, even wherever you have a problem, it shows a place where you have reacted without love. Since the world mirrors your mind, you are only acting that way to yourself. What you see in others is your own private movie projected on the world. It is how you think of yourself, and when you react lovelessly, you deny yourself the love that wants to come to you from others. You react as if the love they extend to you is fear, and fear seems as attractive as love would have been had you not chosen to split off from yourself, project yourself on the world and then deny yourself love.

To have scarcity in any aspect of your life means that you have not forgiven yourself for a time when you were hardhearted. Though your perception has turned this upside down and now others seemed to do it to you, it was the times that you were hardhearted that caused you suffering. It may look to you like others did something to you or did not do something to you that you wished done. Yet, if you were to see your subconscious mind it would show you that you set up the situation to get some kind of payoff that was part of your ego's agenda. Or it was a place you were too frightened to move forward to and needed something to give you the excuse to back away or stop. Your ego's agenda only looks like it will make you happy, but it ends up building the ego. What you have chosen could never make you happy. The independence that you chose was not the liberty you were seeking. It was a role that couldn't receive or enjoy and so it set up other roles of victim and the sacrificer.

Getting attention, specialness, dark glamour, all likewise could not satisfy or requite you. Running from your purpose, control, being right, trying to pay off guilt, avoid fear or hide never worked for happiness.

You framed others with your suffering in order to avoid stepping up and shining. You could have saved them but you ended up using them as your best excuse not to step forward. You will later punish yourself with scarcity and other self-defeating problems to attempt to pay off the guilt that this incident instilled in you. You stay in this dark world because you are afraid of light and love. So, separation and problems abound in your private world and experience.

It is all a movie you are shooting to avoid the love that is your purpose and the grace that wants to be extended to you by Heaven to create a Heaven on earth. You are afraid of love, afraid of yourself and afraid of shining, but this can change as you see what it is that you really want. Love is always calling you and, as it says in *A Course in Miracles*, "Love waits on welcome, not on time." It is time to welcome and invite love into your life. Guilt lasts only as long as you believe in it. It is a way of being hardhearted toward yourself. If you gave it up in regard to yourself, you would give it up in terms of everyone. You would invite love in and invite others and Heaven in also. It would be a different world you would experience to the one you currently see. Love would heal you and give you new life and you would share what you receive, so the love that came to you would be given out in an ever increasing upward spiral of happiness. **If you keep asking yourself what you want**, you will make the right choice, erasing the past and inviting love in. It will heal you and make you happy. What do you want? What do you want?

Chapter 99

The Passive-Aggressor Shadow Figure

All shadows are split off self-concepts that you don't even know are there. They are self-concepts or aspects of the mind that contain a good deal of self-hatred and therefore self-punishment. As well as shadows, you may have self-concepts of being a passive-aggressor. The difference is that the self-concepts have much less self-hatred. In the case of self-concepts, the passive-aggressor seems normal, while a shadow contains heavy self-condemnation, which is why you try to hide it.

Passive aggression is one of the forms of anger. The other forms are attack, withdrawal and being a victim. Passive aggression is sneaky in the sense that when you do it, you can deny even it to yourself, as well as to others. Yet, somewhere inside, you must know that you do it or you could never know what to hide from yourself. Those around you are typically aware of your passive aggression. This form of anger is constantly sniping at others from behind the rocks. You can do this for only so long before others build up so much resentment they bomb the rocks from behind which you snipe. Because of your denial, you feel that you are an innocent victim and can't understand why you are being picked on. Yet, inside and behind all this, there is still the glee that angers and frustrates others.

There is a simple way to heal yourself of passive-aggression. But first it is important to realize that you have this type of trap as a bloody-minded way to stay separate and fight the Oneness of Heaven. This is the rebellion that resists the sweet ecstasy of God's Love that would draw you out of this world and into Heaven. Yet, in spite of the misery you have made, you would rather be the King and Queen of this earth, instead of returning to Love Itself. But you cannot have love or peace if you have attack inside you.

Ask yourself how many shadow figures of the passive-aggressor you have. Line them up in front and to the right of you. Then line up all of the passive-aggressor self-concepts you have in front and to the left of you. Ask yourself what impact they have had on your life. Now, melt them all into one big passive-aggressor. Step up to it; it's a hologram. As you step into it, you will see a doorway. This is a gateway of initiation. Step through it to the other side. In the rare case it's a dark place, call your higher mind to bring the light and clear it up. You can invite anyone you have been especially tormenting and empower them with the light of this place also.

Chapter 100

What You are Trying to Get, Holds You Back

Greed, getting, taking, indulgences, attachments, addictions and idols are all things you attempt to get from outside yourself and which hold you back. The attitude of getting and taking, though common enough in the world, leads to hurt, heartbreak and power struggles. It leads to dependency, such as attachment and holding on, and sooner or later it leads to loss, sadness and disappointment. You are looking for something outside you to make you feel better. You depend on what is outside, and not on yourself and Heaven. Something that comes from within or something you receive doesn't fall into this trap. This attitude of getting from the outside to make yourself happy can grow into things that can cause major problems, such as indulgences, addictions and idols. This attitude fosters a path of consumerism and competition rather than cooperation and creativity. Consumerism makes you weak and unresourceful. This attitude of getting can grow into a craving because it doesn't satisfy the desire and can thus turn into greed. Competition drives the dynamic of power struggle. In other words, you can't have a fight without competition. But it also leads to deadness, as there is withdrawal so as not to lose. Competition actually hides a fear of going forward, under the guise of putting its attention on winning. So besides being frightened and shrinking from going forward, competition locks you into the vicious circle of superiority-inferiority. Sometimes you can be above and sometimes below others, but you won't move beyond control or deadness into partnership.

Many times an attitude of getting or indulgence is compensated for with aspects of hard work and sacrifice, but the split mind keeps you anchored rather than moving forward to greater success.

If you are interested in freeing yourself and moving forward in your evolution and success, you can examine every form of getting and recognize that it is this attitude that holds you back the most. Take an area of getting, such as overeating, being a shopaholic, drinking too much or working too hard, and examine what you are trying to get rather than give. Next examine and reflect on what the self-concepts are that are trying to get satisfied by something outside you, even though this can never succeed. To support these self-concepts you have to attempt to fill their needs. Once you understand the neediness of your self-concepts and their particular brand of consuming, with its inability to fully satisfy or fulfill you, you could decide to let go of the whole getting complex. Alternatively, you could integrate any compensation, along with the form of getting needed to heal the split, and create a new level of confidence. You can choose that this occur or ask Heaven to integrate it for you. Once there is peace and a new wholeness again, choose or ask Heaven that the beliefs and self-concepts also be integrated.

It is important to know that every self-concept has needs as part of its make-up. When you separated to form the self-concept, a need began. This then put you in the mind to get or take, fearing that if you received what you needed you would lose the self-concept that you had made in order to build a separate identity to begin with. You are trying to consume in order to satisfy yourself with an ego strategy that can never work. Your self-concepts were built by separation and lack of love. That is how we built our egos. Where we made the original mistake of acting in a loveless way and blaming it on another, we can now invite love in to bring healing. It is the love that will satisfy us. Love never refuses an invitation or a welcome. So, when you find a place of avarice within you, invite love to come in instead.

Summary

The choice for emotional maturity is the choice for truth. It is also the choice for change, a step toward greater relatedness, success and flow. It is the choice for peace and the realization that whatever has upset us *is in need of healing by us*. If we are not at peace, we cannot respond in a way that moves the situation forward rather than just leading to a fight. Emotional maturity begins with awareness, responsibility and giving up all righteousness, which is a sign of a reaction rather than a response.

Our emotional reactions are everything that is in the way between us and love, the essential aspect of Heaven on earth. An emotion speaks of a wound and it is these wounds that we must heal to become a good partner and not let bullying, need for attention and specialness get in the way of love and the ability to relate.

Emotional maturity leads to ever greater partnership and the restoration of our feminine side. This gives us the ability to receive and enjoy. It returns our loveableness.

Commit again and again to emotional maturity and this alone will heal conflicts of the past. Love and success await you if you are vigilant in regard to emotions and use them for healing. Your wholeness and your peace will grow. Your confidence and power will grow rather than your need to dominate or be victimized. Equality awaits us and with that comes love and helpfulness. Life and success become easy and we begin to unwrap the ego's stranglehold on us, with its desire to make us small and then exaggerate us for its benefit. We begin living under the auspices of our higher mind that is responsive, and the only 'sacrifice' it guides us to is to sacrifice our suffering.